Cultural Olympians

Cultural Olympians
Rugby School's Intellectual and Spiritual Leaders

Edited by
Patrick Derham
and
John Taylor

The University of Buckingham Press

First published in Great Britain in 2013 by

The University of Buckingham Press
Yeomanry House
Hunter Street
Buckingham MK18 1EG

© The Authors

The moral right of the authors has been asserted.

All rights reserved. No part of this publication may be reproduced, stored or introduced into a retrieval system or transmitted in any form or by any means without the prior permission of the publisher nor may be circulated in any form of binding or cover other than the one in which it is published and without a similar condition including this condition being imposed on the subsequent purchaser.

A CIP catalogue record for this book is available at the British Library

The picture of RG Collingwood is reproduced with the kind permission of Magdalen College, Oxford; the picture of TH Green is reproduced with the kind Permission of Balliol College, Oxford. The other images are all provided by and reproduced with the kind permission of Rugby School.

ISBN 978-1-908684-07-3

Printed and bound in Great Britain by
Marston Book Services Limited, Didcot

CONTENTS

Foreword by Rowan Williams

Notes on Contributors

Introduction — i

Thomas Arnold: Legend, Tradition and History — 1
John Witheridge

Archbishop Tait and the Church of the Future — 11
John Clarke

Arthur Hugh Clough and Agnosticism — 27
Anthony Kenny

William Temple: "Confident Living after Careful Prayer" — 45
David Urquhart

Matthew Arnold — 61
Robin Le Poidevin

Lewis Carroll and Victorian Controversy — 75
A N Wilson

T.H. Green: political and philosophical radical — 85
Andrew Vincent

Sidgwick and Hare — 97
A C Grayling

R. H. Tawney: The Making of a Christian socialist — 111
Jay Winter

Frederick Temple and the *Essays and Reviews* Controversy — 123
Ian Hesketh

RG Collingwood: the Renaissance Man — 137
David Boucher

Foreword

Rowan Williams

These brief but packed and fascinating pieces give us a remarkable picture of a school that has done rather more than its share in shaping the literary, theological and educational culture of England over a century and a half. Rugby began its life as the flagship for a new and more morally intense view of what education for the sons of the comfortable and powerful should be in this country. We may smile or even frown at some of the more naive or more repressive aspects of what Arnold created; but we should not forget what a chaotic and lethargic educational world he came into and what an immense impact his work had in redefining a national vision that refused to leave the comfortable and powerful without some tough challenges as to how they could share their comfort and use their power.

From its beginnings, Rugby sought to hold on to a conviction that education was about forming character – not in the bland sense of inculcating a package of individual virtues, but as a means of shaping civic and public agents who lived their lives in steady awareness of having to give an answer for their choices and policies. The vision was about what it means to be responsible – before God, yes, but also to and for others, not least those who could not defend themselves, a deeply important part of the Arnoldian legacy. From Arnold to the Temples and Tawney and beyond, this continued to be the ground bass of the music. This book appropriately celebrates this legacy; and it ought to prompt some hard questions about where any comparable moral, social and imaginative energy is generated in our educational policies today.

+Rowan Williams, Magdalene College, Cambridge

Notes on Contributors

Rowan Williams

Rowan Williams was born in South Wales and studied theology at Cambridge. After research at Oxford in Russian religious thought, he taught at the College of the Resurrection, Mirfield, and then returned to Cambridge for nine years of academic and parish work. In 1986, he was elected Lady Margaret Professor of Divinity at Oxford, and in 1992 became Bishop of Monmouth. He was Archbishop of Wales from 1999 to 2002, and Archbishop of Canterbury from 2002 to 2012. He has written a number of books on theology and spirituality, as well as many essays on contemporary issues and four volumes of poetry. He is now Master of Magdalene College, Cambridge.

John Witheridge

The Reverend John Witheridge specialised in Church History at Christ's College, Cambridge where he was Tancred Divinity Student. He was ordained in 1979 and served his curacy at Luton Parish Church. He has been Head of Religious Studies at Marlborough, Chaplain to the Archbishop of Canterbury, Hon. Curate at St Martin-in-the-Fields, Conduct (Senior Chaplain) of Eton, and, since 1996, Headmaster of Charterhouse. He is the author of various theological articles and reviews. His book on Sir Frank Fletcher (2005) was described by D.R. Thorpe as 'The best account of a Head Master's life and his times since Noel Annan's classic biography of Roxburgh of Stowe.' His authorised biography of Arthur Stanley, Thomas Arnold's biographer, is to be published in 2013.

John Clarke

John Clarke read history at Wadham College and graduated with first class honours. He was then elected to a Prize Fellowship at All Souls College. In the early 1970s, he completed his doctorate on social and economic history in the early 19th century. Professor Clarke has published books on *George III (1972)*, *England in the Age of Cobbett (1977)*, *British Diplomacy and Foreign Policy (1989)* as well as others on local history. Professor Clarke has been associated with the University of Buckingham from the start of the project in 1976. He was Dean of Admissions and Senior Lecturer in History. He became Professor of History in 1999. John Clarke has taught undergraduates at Wadham, Brasenose, Worcester, Balliol, St Hugh's and St John's Colleges in Oxford and has also supervised the work of several graduate students.

Anthony Kenny

Anthony Kenny, having returned to the lay state after seven years as a Roman Catholic priest, became in 1963 Fellow and Tutor in Philosophy at Balliol College in Oxford. He was later Master of that College and subsequently Warden of Rhodes House. He served as President of the British Academy and as Chair of the Board of the British Library. In addition to many books on philosophy he has written a biography of Arthur Hugh Clough, whose Oxford diaries he edited.

David Urquhart

David Urquhart is the 9th Bishop of Birmingham, inaugurated in 2006. From Rugby School, he volunteered in Idi Amin's Uganda where he became a committed Christian. After ten years in the oil industry, based in London, and theological study at Oxford, he was ordained, aged 32, to parishes in inner city Hull, later serving in Coventry and Birkenhead.

As a bishop in the Church of England, in the largest UK city outside London, he is actively involved with education, industry and commerce. Chair of the Birmingham Social Inclusion Process, he is passionate about social and economic justice. David promotes inter-faith 'presence and engagement' in one of the UK's most ethnically diverse regions, and is an enthusiastic practitioner of ecumenical Christian mission.

A former Chair of the Church Mission Society he maintains close links with DR Congo, Uganda and Malawi. He is the Archbishop of Canterbury's Envoy to China, Chair of Ridley Hall, Cambridge, a Church Commissioner and a member of the House of Lords

Robin Le Poidevin

Robin Le Poidevin is Professor of Metaphysics at the University of Leeds, where he has taught since 1989. He was educated at Repton and Oriel College, Oxford, and took a doctorate in philosophy at Emmanuel College,

Cambridge. He has been Gifford Fellow in Philosophy and Natural Theology at St Andrews, Stanton Lecturer in the Philosophy of Religion at Cambridge, and Richardson Fellow in Theology at Durham. He is the editor of *Religious Studies*, and his publications include *Arguing for Atheism* (1996), *Travels in Four Dimensions* (2003), *The Images of Time* (2007) and *Agnosticism: A Very Short Introduction* (2010). He is currently writing a book on the Incarnation and contemporary metaphysics.

A N Wilson

A. N. Wilson attended Rugby School from 1964-1968 and went on to New College Oxford, where he later taught English Language and Literature for seven years. He subsequently became Literary Editor of The Spectator and The Evening Standard. His books on the Victorian era include *God's Funeral* (an account of the Victorian crisis of faith) *The Victorians* and, a novel - *Gentlemen in England*. All these books reflect the interests which animate his contribution here on Lewis Carroll. His latest book is a novel based on the life of Josiah Wedgwood - *The Potter's Hand*.

Andrew Vincent

Andrew Vincent is Honorary Professor of Political Philosophy, Cardiff University and Emeritus Professor, Sheffield University; Professorial Fellow of the Collingwood and British Idealism Centre, Cardiff University; Fellow of the Royal Historical Society; Fellow of the Learned Society of Wales; co-Director of the Political Studies Association British Idealism Specialist Group; previously Senior Research Fellow on several occasions in Australian National University; Visiting Professor at Chinese University Hong Kong; author or co-author of eleven books and three edited collections and over seventy articles. Book publications include: *Philosophy, Politics and Citizenship* (1984), *Theories of the State* (1987), *Modern Political Ideologies* (1993, 3rd edition 2010):); *A Radical Hegelian: The Political and Social Philosophy of Henry Jones* (1993) and *British Idealism and Political Theory* (both co-authored with David Boucher) (2001); *Nationalism and Particularity* (2002); *The Nature of Political Theory* (winner of the Political Studies Association UK Mackenzie Book prize for best book published 2004); *The Politics of Human Rights* (2010); *British Idealism: A Guide to the Perplexed* (co-authored with David Boucher) (2011); *Comparative Political Thought: Theorizing Practices* (co-edited with Michael

Freeden) (2012); *Liberalism and Human Rights* (co-authored with David Boucher) (2013).

A C Grayling

A. C. Grayling M.A., DPhil (Oxon) FRSL is Master of the New College of the Humanities, London, and Professor of Philosophy there. He taught at Oxford and London universities before his present position, and remains a Supernumerary Fellow of St Anne's College, Oxford. He is the author of over 20 books on philosophy and other subjects and a frequent contributor to the press and broadcast media on matters of public concern.

Jay Winter

Jay Winter was a Fellow of Pembroke College, Cambridge, and Lecturer, then Reader of Modern History at Cambridge from 1979-2001. He is now the Charles J. Stille Professor of History at Yale University. He is the author of *Sites of Memory, Sites of Mourning: The Great War in European Cultural History* (Cambridge University Press, 1995); *Remembering War* (Yale University Press, 2006) and *Dreams of Peace and Freedom* (Yale University Press, 2006). His biography *René Cassin et les droits de l'homme*, co-authored with Antoine Prost, was published by Fayard in February 2011. The English version will appear in 2013. He is editor-in-chief of the three-volume Cambridge History of the First World War, to be published in 2014.

Ian Hesketh

Ian Hesketh is a Postdoctoral Research Fellow at the Centre for the History of European Discourses, The University of Queensland, Brisbane, Australia. He is the Assistant Editor of *The Oxford History of Historical Writing*, 5 vols. (Oxford University Press, 2011–2012), and is the author of *The Science of History in Victorian Britain* (Pickering & Chatto, 2011) and *Of Apes and Ancestors: Evolution, Christianity, and the Oxford Debate* (University of Toronto Press, 2009). His research articles have appeared in *History and Theory*, the *Journal of the Canadian Historical Association*, *Victorian Review*, and *Left History*. He is writing a book under contract with the University of Toronto Press entitled "The Manufacturing of a Reluctant Literary Sensation in Victorian Britain: JR Seeley, *Ecce Homo*, and the Historical Jesus" and is currently researching for a monograph project on "Darwin and the Historians: Evolution, Progress, and Purpose in Victorian Historical Writing."

David Boucher

David Boucher is Professor of Political Theory and International Relations at Cardiff University, and Senior Research Associate, University of Johannesburg. He is Chair of the Charitable Trust, The R. G. Collingwood Society, and Director of the R.G. Collingwood and British Idealism Centre, Cardiff. He has published widely in political theory, history of political thought, international relations and cultural studies. His most recent books are *The Limits of Ethics in International Relations* (2009), and *British Idealism: A Guide for the Perplexed* (2011 with Andrew Vincent). He is the author of *The Social and Political Thought of R. G. Collingwood* (1989), and has edited three works by Collingwood. He is currently editing a revised edition of Collingwood's autobiography with Teresa Smith entitled *An Autobiography and Travels in the East Indies* to be published by Oxford University Press in 2013.

Patrick Derham

Patrick Derham has been Head Master of Rugby School since September 2001. After studying History at Cambridge he taught at Cheam and Radley before becoming Head Master of Solihull School in September 1996.

Passionate about widening access Patrick set up the Arnold Foundation for Rugby School in 2003 which provides a boarding education at Rugby to under-privileged children and was instrumental in the setting up of the Springboard Bursary Foundation, a new national charity closely modelled on the Arnold Foundation, in November 2012. He is also Deputy Chairman of Trustees of **Into**University and a Trustee of the Gladstone Library.

Patrick co-edited *Liberating Learning Widening Participation* with Michael Worton, Vice-Provost of UCL, published by UBP in 2010.

John Taylor

John Taylor is Head of Philosophy and Director of Critical Skills at Rugby School. He was educated at Rising Brook High School in Stafford, and at Balliol College, Oxford, where he read Physics and Philosophy. He completed his BPhil and DPhil at Balliol, working in the philosophy of science. He taught in various Oxford colleges and was an Adjunct Lecturer in Philosophy for the International Study Centre of Queen's University. He has taught at Rugby School since 1999. He directed the Perspectives on Science project and is a Chief Examiner for the Extended Project Qualification. He has been a contributing author and co-editor of a number of textbooks and in 2012 he published 'Think Again: A Philosophical Approach to Teaching'. He is a Visiting Fellow of the Institute of Education.

Introduction

Patrick Derham and John Taylor

The liberal tradition is one which values openness to a plurality of viewpoints and is committed to the use of reasoned enquiry and dialogue in the context of disagreement. Liberalism stems from a recognition of the difficulty of establishing certainty when addressing the questions of history, philosophy and ethics. Consequently, the tradition places emphasis on the importance of what Keats called "negative capability": the ability to live, creatively and confidently, in the face of uncertainty, and to utilize this uncertainty as a spur to fresh thinking and engagement with the deepest questions of all.

The educational importance of liberalism should be self-evident, though, in an age when education has come increasingly to be valued for instrumental or utilitarian reasons, it is in constant need of being re-stated and defended. In recent years, we have aimed to mount a two-pronged attack: to argue vigorously in defence of the liberal approach, and to demonstrate, by engagement in curriculum reform, that its ideals can be implemented in ways which are practical and functional. [1] We have sought, both in theory and practice, to advocate a philosophical approach to education.

Education, on this view of things, is the project of enabling young people to consider, and answer in their own lives, the great question of Socrates: "how, then, should we live?" It is, through and through, an ethical enterprise. It is also an enterprise premised on the application of critical, reflective enquiry ("the unconsidered life is not worth living", as Socrates remarked, in partial answer to his own question) and on the task of humbly attending to the best that has been said and thought on the question, as Matthew Arnold would have it.

---

[1] See Derham and Worton (2010) *Liberating Learning, Widening Participation* (University of Buckingham Press) and Taylor (2011) *Think Again: A Philosophical Approach to Teaching* (Continuum)

Liberal education is a response to a fact about the human condition: the fact that when we engage in the project of reflection on life itself, we find that questions mount up more quickly than answers. Nowhere is this truer than in the sphere of the humanities. About matters of history, ethics, theology and metaphysics, we find the desire for certainty thwarted by the limitations of our human faculties, by the confusion of our language and by the fact that even our best thinking is bound to find itself conditioned by presupposition, tradition and context. The desire for absolute certainty, which Descartes made central to the tradition of modern Western thought, is one which is destined necessarily to be frustrated.

Knowledge of how to live with uncertainty is one of the best lessons that liberal education affords. An acknowledgement that, in the pursuit of religious, ethical, philosophical or historical truth, our best thinking falls short of achieving finality engenders the virtues of humility, tolerance and empathy. But, crucially, the fact that we consider ourselves to be fallible in the pursuit of truth presupposes the idea that truth remains as our goal. The sceptics of antiquity saw themselves as those who seek; they aimed not to create a climate of crippling doubt, but to engender an ongoing quest for truth. Moreover, if objective truth, by its nature, will never be attainable with finality, the quest will be one which is always open to a new generation. We may climb high, and perceive new horizons, but beyond these, yet further horizons remain undiscovered.

It was with these thoughts in mind that we decided to turn for inspiration to some of those former members of our School whose lives and thought embodied greatness in the sphere of cultural endeavour. In focussing on pioneers who were all pupils or teachers at Rugby School, there is a danger of succumbing to a certain parochialism; to imply that, so to speak, something rather special in the waters of East Warwickshire caused a flowering of talent and an influence which extended across the globe. It is not our intention to advance any such thesis. Instead, our intention is simply to bring together, in illuminating juxtaposition, accounts of the lives and thought of some of those Rugbeians who gained a reputation for cultural, intellectual and spiritual leadership: the "cultural olympians" of their day. The lives of those whose stories are recounted here have much that is interesting and, perhaps, instructive to say.

These stories are, we believe, of more than purely historical interest. They promise to shed light on some of the complexities of the ongoing process of grappling with such matters as the relationship between faith and knowledge, the foundation of ethics within a largely secular, pluralist society, the nature of historical understanding, the challenge of social inequality, the priority of religious practice over doctrine – and, summing these up, at the most simple and profound level – the way in which we should go about answering Socrates' great question of how should we live.

Aside from their connection to Rugby School, is there a common thread which runs through the lives of our cultural olympians? It would be mistaken to characterize them all as holders of a set of shared philosophical doctrines. But perhaps they can fruitfully be seen as sharing a way of addressing the great questions of their day. Imaginative, creative engagement with uncertainty – Keat's negative capability – is recognizable as an element in the mindset of our cultural olympians. We offer this thought, not as a thesis, but as an hypothesis to be held in mind when reading the chapters which follow.

We can perhaps also discern a shared outlook amongst Rugby's cultural olympians. Their liberal mindset is one which respected the need for critical, reflective, informed enquiry, but also allowed for openness to the insights which can be gained from traditional outlooks, and respect for the religious sensibility. It was an approach which connected creative thought about the transcendent with humility about the limitations of knowledge.

If not informed by an appropriate philosophical understanding, discussion of these topics is apt to degenerate into an intemperate exchange between dogmatically opposed positions, or, conversely, to wither away under the influence of the relativistic assumption that there is no objective truth to be pursued. By contrast, the form of reflective questioning described in the chapters that follow offers a paradigm for liberal, philosophically-oriented enquiry into matters of ultimate significance, about which there remains deep-seated disagreement.

Thomas Arnold: Legend, Tradition and History

John Witheridge

A witty school novel entitled *The Lanchester Tradition* was published a few months before the outbreak of the First World War. Its author was G.F. Bradby, son of Dr E.H. Bradby, a pupil under Arnold who returned after Balliol to teach at Rugby, before becoming Master of Haileybury. He sent his three sons to Rugby, two of whom also became masters. In 1900, the younger, A.C. Bradby, wrote about Rugby for the Handbooks to the Great Public Schools series, and described Arnold as "perhaps the most famous of schoolmasters; everyone has heard of him; at Rugby his name is still on all lips."[1] The Bradby brothers were steeped in the Arnold tradition which G.F. satirises in *The Lanchester Tradition*. It is about the staff of Chiltern School, and the trials and tribulations which beset a new, reforming headmaster. Despite his protestations that "the masters and boys who figure in the following pages have never existed outside the author's brain",[2] Chiltern is evidently Rugby, and Abraham Lanchester is Thomas Arnold. In the minds of at least some of the masters, his writ (or at least their version of it) still runs:

> In spite of its ancient school-rooms, noble grounds, and salubrious climate, Chiltern would probably never have become one of the public schools of England if it had not been for Dr. Lanchester . . . Chiltern has lived ever since on (his) memory . . . The Lanchester tradition permeates the place like an atmosphere, invisible but stimulating . . . Any change in the hour of a lesson or the colour of a ribbon is regarded as an outrage on the Lanchester tradition, and is popularly supposed to make the dead hero turn in his grave.[3]

The Chiltern masters revere Lanchester as their "second and greater founder",[4] but much of what they admire is a caricature. Some matters, like the detail of uniform or the structure of the timetable, which they regard as important, had either been of little interest to Lanchester, or were later innovations which he would not even have recognised, let alone preserved.

All this is also entirely true of Arnold at Rugby. Like his counterpart, Arnold had been a restless reformer who had fought hard to change and improve a school he found ossified by custom and neglect. He has also, like Lanchester, acquired a posthumous reputation which mingles fact and fiction, history and legend, and in which, furthermore, the legendary, fictional aspects have come to dominate the tradition and the popular image. To understand why and how this has occurred we need to consider and compare three influential sources for Arnold's life. The first is Arthur Stanley's two volume *Life and Correspondence* (1844); the second, Thomas Hughes's schoolboy classic, *Tom Brown's Schooldays* (1857); and the third,

---

[1] A.C. Bradby, *Rugby* (1900), p. 54.
[2] G.F. Bradby, Preface to *The Lanchester Tradition* (1914).
[3] *Ibid.*, 1954 edn, pp. 13f.
[4] *Ibid.*, p. 13.

Lytton Strachey's essay in *Eminent Victorians* (1918). Stanley's is a serious Victorian biography of nearly 800 pages; the other two are light and readable, and hugely popular in their time. They also depict an Arnold whose characteristics became the stuff of legend.

Stanley's biography is the most historically authentic and reliable source. As a boy at Rugby, Stanley had idolised Arnold, and Arnold regarded him as "the almost perfect example of the kind of boy he hoped the school would produce."[5] He was precociously intelligent and bookish, and was taught by Arnold for three years in the sixth form, putting him in daily touch with Arnold's thoughts and ideals. His biography is sympathetic, certainly, but objective and detached, and deliberately not a panegyric. The Arnold Stanley represents is, first and foremost, a prophetic figure, deeply and earnestly Christian, and it is this religious and moral influence above all that he brings to Rugby. "His great object", wrote Stanley, was "the hope of making the school a place of really Christian education."[6] Arnold's methods, according to Stanley, were his own heroic example of a man always trying to act as in the presence of God; his weekly, spellbinding sermons, more often than not on the struggle with evil and wickedness; teaching, especially of history, which sought to draw moral lessons from the past; stern, but by the standards of the time, humane discipline; and the prefect (praepostor) system, which recruited all thirty members of the sixth to be "actually fellow-workers with him for the highest good of the school".[7] As for the rest of school life, Arnold left it much as he found it. Stanley explains that he really only tinkered with the curriculum, leaving classics to dominate, and refusing to include science. Arnold never took much interest in games, except for an occasional glance out of his study window or stroll around the Close. Besides, organised sport (namely cricket and Rugby's version of football) was still in its infancy, and many of the boys' leisure hours were spent (or wasted) as they had always been, in rambling across the countryside – trespassing, poaching and rat-catching.

Thomas Hughes's *Tom Brown's Schooldays*, published thirteen years after Stanley's *Life*, gives a different picture, though in many respects a complementary one. It is an entertaining adventure story, but written with an

---

[5] Peter Hinchcliff, *Benjamin Jowett and the Christian Religion* (1987), p. 27.
[6] A.P. Stanley, *The Life and Correspondence of Thomas Arnold, D.D.* (1844), 1901 one vol. edn, p. 94.
[7] *Ibid.*, pp. 105f.

evangelical purpose, namely to win admiration for the great Christian headmaster and, through him, to Christ, "who is the King and Lord of heroes".[8] Although Hughes had also been a pupil under Arnold, his novel is in places anachronistic, in that he reads back into Arnold's time some later public school developments, especially the new cult of games, and what became known as 'muscular Christianity'. It is this aspect of the Arnold legend that Hughes bequeaths to the tradition. He was predisposed to do so because, as a boy at Rugby, he had been much like Tom Brown – unintellectual, mischievous and keen on sports. He was not clever enough to join the sixth so never knew Arnold except from afar. It is instructive that when Stanley first read the book he said he was amazed to have discovered aspects of the school of which he had been entirely ignorant.[9] What Stanley did recognise as authentic though was the story's depiction of how supremely important Arnold was to his pupils, and especially how they thought and felt when they heard of his death.[10]

The Arnold of *Eminent Victorians* is the product of the fashionable anti-public school prejudice which followed the First World War. "Arnold and Arnold's Rugby were easy targets for the anti-Victorian sniper", wrote Basil Willey, and Stanley's Arnold is "a high-minded but blundering and conventional prig".[11] Strachey's essay represents a cynical reworking of the Arnold of Hughes's fiction, supported by selective treatment of Stanley's facts. In so doing, Strachey adds two more dimensions to the Arnold legend – that he was a typical Victorian, eminent or otherwise, and that he had ruled Rugby by fear, as Keate ruled Eton by flogging.[12] "As the Israelite of old knew that his almighty Lawgiver might at any moment thunder to him from the whirlwind, or appear before his very eyes, the visible embodiment of power or wrath, so the Rugby schoolboy walked in a holy dread of some sudden manifestation of the sweeping gown, the majestic tone, the piercing glance, of Dr Arnold."[13]

---

[8] Thomas Hughes, *Tom Brown's Schooldays* (1857), Puffin Classics edn, 1994, p. 371.
[9] See *The Spectator*, 6 November 1897, at 645.
[10] See address in Rugby School Chapel, 12 June 1874; *Macmillan's Magazine*, July 1874, xxx (May-October 1874), at 279.
[11] Basil Willey, *Nineteenth Century Studies* (1949), pp. 59f.
[12] John Keate, Head Master of Eton (1809-34), was notorious for the severity of his discipline. His old-fashioned methods were in stark contrast to Arnold's.
[13] Lytton Strachey, *Eminent Victorians* (1918), Penguin Modern Classics edn, 1975, p. 168.

These are also fictions not facts. First, Arnold was not a Victorian. He was born in 1795 when George III was King, and was in his teens and twenties during the Regency. Only his last five years were lived during the reign of Queen Victoria, and he died twenty years before Prince Albert. He taught Victorians, and his ideals and methods laid Victorian foundations, but he was not himself a Victorian. Second, though Arnold may have been by nature serious, and though he lived in a time when a great gulf was fixed between schoolmasters and their charges, Stanley and Hughes both depict Arnold as a fond father who was essentially compassionate and kind to his pupils. Stanley says that "the recollections of the head-master of Rugby are inseparable from the recollections of the personal guide and friend of his scholars."[14] He speaks too of "a deep undercurrent of sympathy which extended to almost all, and which from time to time broke through the reserve of his outward manner."[15] In *Tom Brown's Schooldays*, Arnold arranges for Tom to share a study with George Arthur, a new boy who was likely to find life at Rugby a trial.[16] Tom rises to the challenge, encourages the boy, and protects him from the bullies. On his last day, a master explains to Tom what the Doctor had intended, and describes "'the care with which he has watched over every step in your school lives.'"[17] Would so many of Arnold's pupils have loved and revered him as they did if this had not been true?

So much for the legends; what now of history?

Arnold's religion was a curious mixture of simple, unquestioning, almost Evangelical convictions about sin and salvation, and an independent-minded and critical approach to truth, which exposed almost everything else to the light of history and reason. The former derived as much from his temperament as his upbringing, and the latter from four years as a fellow of Oriel College, Oxford, and the company he kept there with a group of clever, liberal dons nicknamed the Noetics. Oriel also introduced Arnold to the theological writings of Samuel Taylor Coleridge to which the Noetics turned for inspiration, and whose son, Hartley, was also a fellow. A variety of doctrinal doubts prevented Arnold from being ordained priest until his appointment to Rugby in 1828.

---

[14] Stanley, *op.cit.*, p. 122.
[15] *Ibid.*, p. 154
[16] Supposed to be Arthur Stanley, though Hughes refuted any suggestion that his characters (apart from Arnold) were modelled on particular persons.
[17] Hughes, *op.cit.*, p. 359.

Arnold was an historian not a theologian, though the distinctions between the two disciplines were not as clearly defined then as they are now. In both he displayed a radical and pioneering streak.

Before Rugby Arnold had run a small private school at Laleham, and it was there that he learned German in order to read the works of the historian Barthold Niebuhr. In his *Roman History*, Niebuhr had been the first to apply the new critical method on a grand scale, a method that was becoming indispensable to the pursuit of historical truth. Arnold's admiration for Niebuhr was unbounded, and he recognised in him the same union as his own of deep religious conviction and uncompromising liberalism. Niebuhr's great work inspired and shaped Arnold's own three volume *History of Rome* (1838-42).[18] Arnold's genius as an historian can be seen here in his independence of judgement, his appreciation of geography's bearing on history, and his capacity for military exposition. Also present is Arnold's deep sense of the historian's moral duty: "no student or writer of history has ever been more conscious than Arnold of the responsibility implied in Acton's memorable saying that 'if we lower our standard on History, we cannot uphold it in Church and State.'"[19] In 1841, the year before he died, Arnold was appointed Regius Professor of Modern History at Oxford. The Sheldonian Theatre was packed for his inaugural lecture, in which he challenged any hard and fast boundary between the civilisation of Greece and Rome, and the progress of modern history.

In addition to six volumes of sermons, Arnold published two important and controversial theological pamphlets, *On the Right Interpretation and Understanding of the Scriptures* (1832) and *Principles of Church Reform* (1833). In the former, Arnold drew on the new historical critical approach to the Bible, also pioneered in Germany, and he followed Coleridge in distinguishing between questions of criticism and questions of religion. The second, he argues, are the important questions, because the true basis of religion is moral and spiritual, not historical or scientific. "We hear a great deal, he says, of historical, critical and scientific 'objections' to the Bible, and it seems to be

---

[18] Arnold had already written a short unpublished history of Greece and a series of articles on Roman history, published posthumously. He also produced a three volume edition of Thucydides.

[19] Sir A.W. Ward and A.R. Waller (eds), *The Cambridge History of English Literature* (1970), xii.1, p. 303: Acton's saying is from his inaugural lecture as Professor of Modern History at Cambridge, *On the Study of History* (1895).

supposed that the Christian faith depends upon their solution, whereas it is really quite unconcerned with them."[20] Coleridge's influence is evident again in *Principles of Church Reform*. Arnold challenges any separation of Church from society (or from State or nation or school). In God's world, all things are at once spiritual and secular, sacred and profane. Such a separation means, on the one hand, the surrender of all temporal concerns to the devil, and on the other, the retreat of religion into sectarianism, and what Arnold called 'priestcraft', by which he meant the introspective sacerdotal world of ritual, ceremony and superstition.[21] Instead, the true purpose of the Church is to be "a society for the purpose of making men like Christ,—earth like heaven,—the kingdoms of the world the kingdom of Christ."[22] The Church of England, as the national Church, is in a strong and privileged position "to Christianise the nation, and introduce the principles of Christianity into men's social and civil relations."[23] To that end, Arnold argued that the Church of England should become more comprehensive by including Nonconformists and giving greater responsibility to the laity.

During his lifetime, Arnold's reputation had been for his theological opinions, which were deemed radical enough to prevent any preferment in the Church. His sudden death in 1842, the day before his forty-seventh birthday, raised his profile. Stanley's biography, published just two years later, brought his work as headmaster to public attention, and won for him an admiration and respect he had not enjoyed before.

Stanley emphasised three aspects of Arnold as headmaster: Christianiser, teacher and ruler. As Christianiser, Arnold brought to bear in the microcosm of Rugby his ideal of the Church. "The idea of a Christian school", wrote Stanley, "was to him the natural result, so to speak, of the very idea of a school in itself; exactly as the idea of a Christian State seemed to him to be involved in the very idea of a State itself."[24] The school Arnold inherited, like every public school at the time, was marred by poor conditions, unruly behaviour, and severe punishments. Arnold regarded boys' bad behaviour as

---

[20] Willey, *op.cit.*, p. 76.
[21] This is how Arnold regarded the Oxford Movement, and why he was so vehement in his opposition: see his essay on 'The Oxford Malignants', *Edinburgh Review*, April 1836.
[22] Arnold to J.T. Coleridge, November 18th 1835, quoted by Stanley, *op.cit.*, p. 387.
[23] Quoted by Stanley, *ibid.*, p. 243.
[24] *Ibid.*, p. 95.

grave sinfulness, and he used his Sunday afternoon sermons to identify and challenge it, and to urge his pupils to follow instead the example of Christ. "It was of course in their direct practical application to the boys that the chief novelty and excellence of his sermons consisted . . . It was the man himself, there more than in any other place . . . combating face to face the evil, with which directly or indirectly he was elsewhere perpetually struggling . . . (and) labouring to win others to share in his own personal feelings of disgust at sin, and love of goodness, and to trust in the same faith, in which he hoped to live and die himself."[25] This is Stanley's description and Hughes's is much the same.[26]

Stanley returned to Rugby in 1874 to address the school on the thirty-second anniversary of Arnold's death:

> What was it that Arnold told us of Religion? It was that Religion—the relation of the soul to God—depends on our own moral and spiritual characters. He made us understand that the only one thing for which God supremely cares, the only thing God supremely loves is goodness—that the only thing which is supremely hateful to God is wickedness. All other things are useful, admirable, beautiful in their several ways. All forms, ordinances, means of instruction, means of amusement, have their place in our lives. But Religion, the true Religion of Jesus Christ, consists in that which makes us wiser and better, more truthful, more loving, more tender, more considerate, more pure. Therefore, in his view, there was no place or time from which Religion is shut out—there is no place or time where we cannot be serving God by serving our fellow-creatures.[27]

Stanley also asked in his address what Arnold had taught of history. His answer was that he made his pupils feel that the dead men of Greece and Rome, and the departed times of England and France, were full of living interest. He made them understand the greatness of Christianity by making them feel the grandeur of Europe and the magnificence of Christendom. He helped them to understand religion through knowledge of the successive forms which goodness and truth can take at different times. Above all, Arnold showed how the study of the past taught moral lessons, and

---

[25] *Ibid.*, pp. 145, 147f.
[26] See Hughes, *op.cit.*, pp. 143ff.
[27] *Macmillan's Magazine*, *op.cit.*, at 279.

furthermore, "no direct instruction could leave on their minds a livelier image of his disgust at moral evil, than the black cloud of indignation which passed over his face when speaking of the crimes of Napoleon, or of Caesar, and of the dead pause which followed, as if the acts had just been committed in his very presence."[28]

Arnold brought order to Rugby by means of his domineering personality and example, the high moral standards he set, the sense of purpose and habits of hard work he instilled, the use of the birch or expulsion when necessary, and his reorganisation and deployment of praepostors. His insistence that the prefect body should consist of the clever boys of the sixth, who were taught almost entirely by himself, was designed to provide informed and enlightened leadership. It was, according to Stanley, "the keystone of his whole government".[29] Arnold shared his own high ideals with his prefects, and trusted them to convey his principles to the rest of the school. "They had, with him, a moral responsibility and a deep interest in the real welfare of the place."[30] This close, pastoral relationship that Arnold nurtured with the sixth was unheard of in an age when boys and masters inhabited entirely different, indeed alien worlds of mutual mistrust.

School trustees who had read Stanley's biography were determined to appoint men as headmasters who had been pupils or masters under Arnold, and this led to an extraordinary colonisation. Over twenty public schools in the second half of the nineteenth century were led, and reformed, by Arnold's disciples. The Provost of Oriel's famous testimonial that "if Mr. Arnold were elected to the head-mastership of Rugby, he would change the face of education all through the public schools of England"[31] could not have been more prescient. This remarkable dissemination of Arnold's ideal and methods certainly strengthened the public schools, and the grammar schools too which followed in their wake. But it also added legends to the Arnold tradition. A school with an Arnoldian as its headmaster could easily confuse its non-Arnoldian features with Arnold's influence (along the lines of *The Lanchester Tradition*). Furthermore, it could be tempting for headmasters like these to collude with this, either in order to defend the status quo, or to validate reforms of their own devising. This is certainly the

---

[28] Stanley, *op.cit.*, p. 132.
[29] *Ibid.*, p. 105.
[30] *Ibid.*, p. 106.
[31] *Ibid.*, p. 49: the Provost was Edward Hawkins.

case, for instance, with George Cotton at Marlborough, who outlawed the boys' popular jaunts across the Wiltshire downs and replaced them instead with compulsory team games. This had been almost unknown to him at Rugby, at least while Arnold was headmaster, but he was astute enough to allow Arnold to take the credit.[32]

---

[32] Cotton had been engaged to Arnold's daughter but broke off the engagement the month before the wedding. Arnold never recovered from the distress and disappointment.

Archbishop Tait and the Church of the Future

John Clarke

Arnold's successor as Headmaster of Rugby was Archibald Campbell Tait, later Dean of Carlisle, Bishop of London and finally Archbishop of Canterbury. Tait had been born in Edinburgh in 1811 and grew up in the Church of Scotland. In 1830, however, he moved south to study at Balliol College, Oxford, where he became a Fellow in 1834. While at Balliol, Tait was confirmed into the Church of England, becoming a

Deacon in 1836 and Priest in 1838.[1] Tait exemplifies a distinct phase in the history of the Church of England. For the first time since the sixteenth century, the headship of a famous School was seen as an ideal stepping stone to the highest offices in the Church. Of the eight Archbishops of Canterbury appointed in the hundred years after 1860, six had previously been public school headmasters[2] and four had Rugby associations.[3] Even the non-Headmaster Archbishops – Randall Davidson[4] and Cosmo Gordon Lang – shared important characteristics with Tait. Like him, both were born in Scotland and Lang was educated at Balliol. The fact that several subsequent Archbishops had so much in common with Tait suggests that "The Tait model" worked so well that it was decided to copy it as closely as possible. Perhaps this in itself is enough to make Tait a Cultural Olympian.

But can any post, however grand - Archbishop of Canterbury or even Headmaster of Rugby - confer Olympian status, *ex-officio* as it were? Both in his life and subsequently, many would have denied Tait any such accolade. The title of the best modern work on Tait, Peter Marsh's *The Victorian Church in Decline: Archbishop Tait and the Church of England, 1868-1882* (1969), hardly suggests admiration. In case we have not grasped the thrust of his thesis – that under Tait's leadership the Church became increasingly marginalised, losing much of the influence it had enjoyed in mid-Victorian England – Marsh calls his first chapter, "From Strength", and his last, "Pushed Aside." Marsh does not say that this was all Tait's fault – but he clearly thinks that some of it was: "Tait's attempt throughout his leadership to bring the Church abreast with the nation left the Church bruised and intensified its preoccupation with its own well-being." [5]

But if Tait was such a disaster, why was he allowed to rise so high? Marsh offers a somewhat distasteful explanation: whenever Tait's career was becalmed or he faced acute difficulty, something dreadful happened to him

---

[1] A C Bickley, *Archibald Campbell Tait: a Sketch of the Public Life of the late Archbishop of Canterbury,* London, 1882, pp. 4-5.
[2] Longley, Tait, Benson, Frederick Temple, William Temple and Fisher. See J. R. de S Honey *Tom Brown's Universe; the Development of the Victorian Public School,* London, 1977, pp. 319, 403.
[3] The Headmaster-Archbishops without Rugby associations were Longley (Harrow) and Fisher (Repton).
[4] Davidson was also Tait's son-in-law and biographer.
[5] Peter T. Marsh, 'Tait, Archibald Campbell', in *ODNB,* vol. 53, p. 657.

and he then "milked" the ensuing sympathy, particularly royal sympathy, to his own advantage. It seems that the pattern began at Rugby. According to Marsh, "the appointment did not prove felicitous." While Tait threw everything into his task, compared to his predecessor, he was remote in manner and inclined to restrain the school-boy fervour Arnold had aroused. Thus Tait only became popular towards the end of his time at Rugby, when a bout of rheumatic fever brought him to death's door, and "concern for the health of the Headmaster stopped an incipient rebellion by the junior school against the sixth."[6] The pattern was repeated, more dramatically, when Tait was at Carlisle. Tait and his wife lost five of their seven children - girls between two and ten years old – to scarlet fever in the space of little more than a month: "from the Queen down, the country was moved at its tenderest point." Queen Victoria insisted that Tait be offered the next vacant bishopric; this turned out to be London, a very senior post, usually given to a man who had already proved himself in a lesser diocese. [7] It happened again in 1878 when Tait lost his wife and son:

> The Archbishop, aged beyond his sixty-six years, sought consolation in preparing a memoir of his wife and son for publication. It was accompanied with almost unbearable pathos by an account Mrs Tait had written twenty years earlier about the death of her five daughters. The book still stands like a great funerary sculpture on the literary landscape of Victorian England. The Archbishop's terrible familiarity with death protected him from personal attack and curbed criticism of his policies.[8]

In the case of many eminent Victorians, the best antidote to the criticisms or innuendos of a Strachey or his equivalent is to turn to a massive but flattering "official" biography produced not long after the death of the subject. At first sight, there is such a source for Tait, so much so that Marsh warns us not to be taken in by it: "Tait has been well served, a bit too well served by his official biographers, William Benham and Randall Davidson."[9] In reality, however, the official life does little to advance Tait's claim to

---

[6] Marsh in *ODNB,* vol. 53, p. 652.
[7] *Ibid.*
[8] Marsh in *ODNB* vol. 53 p. 657.
[9] P. T. Marsh, *The Victorian Church in Decline: Archbishop Tait and the Church of England,* London, 1969, p 11. Marsh is referring to W. Benham and R. T. Davidson, *Life of Archibald Campbell Tait,* London, 2 vols, 1891.

Olympian status. It is not much concerned with cultural matters and, when it was being written, its chief author, Randall Davidson, Tait's son-in-law and fellow Scot, was well on the way to becoming Archbishop of Canterbury himself – and hence reluctant to tackle difficult issues head on. In any case, major figures in the story, such as Queen Victoria and Mr Gladstone, were still alive and needed to be handled with care. In short, if Marsh is too hostile, Benham and Davidson are too bland to offer a convincing assessment of Tait.

Yet the little-known work by Bickley provides a long list of the things Tait was not, before giving a few clues about what he was:

> Dr Tait's claims to the title of a great ecclesiastic are not, perhaps, in some respects, so large as those of some of his predecessors. He was not a statesman like Dunstan, or a patriot like Stephen Langton, or even a theologian like Anselm, but he was the model of a hardworking and judicious Prelate, of a tolerant, earnest and philanthropic clergyman, and a pious and blameless servant of Christ; and he was, in the opinion of Dean Stanley – no mean authority – "the greatest Archbishop since Tillotson."[10]

One wonders whether Bickley understood the significance of what he was saying. His truly great Archbishops – Dunstan, Langton and Anselm - all belong to the centuries before the Reformation; in other words, they were leaders of the Church in England, not of the Church of England. Only Tillotson, William III's Archbishop, represents the post-Reformation Church. Perhaps without realising it Bickley identifies two great traditions:

    I.   those, like Dunstan, Langton and Anselm, who see the English Church as part of that Church that has been Christ's presence and to some extent His body in the world since the Ascension of His body into Heaven; and

---

[10] A. C. Bickley, *Archibald Campbell Tait, A Sketch of the Public Life of the Late Archbishop of Canterbury*. London, 1882, p. 143.

II. those, like Tillotson, who see the Church, first and foremost, as the Church by law established, subject to the jurisdiction of the Crown and of the king in Parliament.[11]

The tradition of Dunstan, Langton and Anselm, may be called "Universalist" or "Catholic." It is harder to put a label on the Tillotson tradition, although "National," or even "Liberal" are reasonable candidates. Despite the obvious tensions between them, both traditions were present in the Church of England of the 1830s. The chief representative of the "Universalist" tradition was John Henry Newman and the chief representative of the "National" or "Liberal" position was Dr Thomas Arnold. Stanley's comparison between Tait and Tillotson leaves us in no doubt that it was to the "National" rather than to the "Universalist" tradition that Tait belonged. When evaluating Tait's claims to greatness, we cannot avoid asking whether he was a worthy opponent of Newman and a worthy successor to Arnold. In fairness to Tait, few would care to be judged in such company or by such standards.

Ironically, it was through Newman that Tait first came to public attention. Newman's *Tract XC* of 1841 represents the limit of how far one can go in the direction of the "Universalist" position and still remain an Anglican. Tait, then a Fellow of Balliol, drew up a "Tutors' Protest" that eventually led the governing Council of the University to condemn *Tract XC* and the Bishop of Oxford to rule that there must be no more Tracts. The condemnation of *Tract XC* was a huge blow to Newman and arguably began the process of alienation that took him to Rome. Many in the Church still deplore the loss of Newman, all the more so because it might have been avoided. Perhaps if Tait had not composed his wretched "Protest," Newman would have stayed where he belonged – in Oxford and in the Church of England. If this evaluation of Tait is right, any claims to Olympian status must be discovered elsewhere.

Tait's role in the suppression of *Tract XC* probably did more than anything else to secure the job at Rugby.[12] Above all it aligned him with

---

[11] J. G. A. Pocock, 'Within the margins – the definition of orthodoxy' in (ed) Roger D. Lund, *The Margins of Orthodoxy; Heterodox writing and cultural response 1660-1750*, Cambridge, 1995, p 37. I am most grateful to Mr Frank Hartley for drawing my attention to this work.

Arnold's attitude to Tractarianism. Had not the Doctor said, "I look upon a Roman Catholic as an enemy in his uniform; I look upon a Tractarian disguised as a spy"? But Arnold had not been exactly flattering about the typical Evangelical either: "a good Christian, with a low understanding, a bad education and ignorance of the world."[13] Before his fatal heart attack in 1842, Arnold was seen as the man most capable of producing an attractive alternative to Tractarianism and Evangelicalism. But with Arnold dead, the challenge increasingly passed to Tait. At the risk of mixing Christian and pagan metaphors, we may say that if Tait deserves admission to Mount Olympus, it must be on the strength of a "National" or "Liberal" entry ticket.

In short, the question is whether Tait could understand, articulate, promote and develop the agenda that Arnold was still formulating at the time of his death – but whose ultimate origins go back to Tillotson? As the lives of men recede further into the past, what they did seems less and less important; what they believed comes to matter much more. For all the attention that has been devoted to Tait, this dimension of the man has been strangely neglected. The time has come to remedy the omission, not least through consideration of his most important work, *The Church of the Future* (1880). If ideas and doctrine really matter, then the most important part of this work is surely the fifth chapter, entitled "Dogmatic Teaching." Tait neatly summarises his position as it might appear to a critic:

> This Church which you are setting before us, for the new age, with its doctrines of the Blessed Trinity, of the corruption of human nature, and the consequent impossibility of man being justified, except through the merits and death of the Lord Jesus Christ, maintaining the old Sacraments and the old ordinances and forms, is nothing else than the old Church of England.[14]

---

[12] It is true that the Balliol of the 1830s was developing a reputation for high-minded earnestness similar to Arnold's ideal. Tait had been Matthew Arnold's tutor at Balliol and was famed for devoting as much attention to the spiritual as to the academic development of his pupils. Even so Tait seems an odd choice for Rugby. His health was poor and he was only thirty years old, unmarried, with no experience of an English Public School and had little charisma.
[13] Quoted in Trevor May, *The Victorian Clergyman,* Oxford, 2006, p. 8.
[14] Archibald Campbell Tait, *The Church of the Future,* London, 1880, p. 133.

Tait insists that what he is looking for is indeed "nothing more or less than the old church of England, freed from certain modern accretions on the one side or the other, which have grown round its authoritative creed in times of deadness or unnatural activity."[15]

> This then, I maintain, is the same reformed old Church of England – Catholic in its connection with antiquity and the Universal Church, Protestant in its opposition to the peculiar encroachments of the Roman See. We think none the worse of it because it is the old English Church which has been tried through severe struggles; which for three hundred years and more has been identified in its present form with the national life; which neither in our fathers' time nor in ours has been the antagonist, but always the ally and patron of learning, of science, and of the nation's growing intelligence. ... while the old churches of East and West cannot refuse it some reverence, and the newer sects feel that it is a bulwark against the return to exploded superstitions; it seems peculiarly pointed out as a centre for union for the long-divided faith of Christians. In it we hold that Christendom has its surest bulwark, both of sound faith and sound morals, against the encroachments of a threatening infidelity.[16]

There are number of key words or phrases in what might be called "Tait's Creed." It is important to understand them, to determine how they fit together and to see how they affect Tait's position on specific issues of the time.

Shortly after becoming Archbishop, Tait was faced with an incoming Liberal government determined to disestablish the Church of Ireland. Such a measure could only work to the advantage of the Roman Catholics, yet Tait felt he must accept it, because the Irish Church enjoyed the loyalty of only a small minority of the people of Ireland. In other words, numbers mattered and, like every other ancient institution in the land, the Church of England was at risk in an age of democracy. Nothing could save the Church of England from the fate of the Church of Ireland if the people of England turned against it and there were many on the Liberal benches eager to proceed to English Disestablishment.

---

[15] *Church of the Future*, p. 134.
[16] *Church of the Future*, pp. 135-6.

For Tait however, the Church of the Future would remain very much an Established Church: "certainly it is our duty to resist all efforts for subverting that national constitution of our Church."[17] It is striking that "Tait's Creed" stresses that the Church of England "has been identified in its present form with the national life." Tait believes that national churches – whether they agree with the Church of England or not – constitute the best antidote to "the encroachments of the Roman see." Above all a National Church becomes the authorised teacher of everyone in that country and "the mouthpiece through which our common Christianity speaks in all our public acts as a state." [18] Thus the National Church is the Church of all even if they do not belong to it and its influence spreads into places where no un-established church could reach. In short, National Churches bring nations a little closer to God.

But it is it is tempting to wonder whether Tait – and indeed other Headmaster/Archbishops - were drawn to Establishment for other reasons. The idea that there could be no sharp distinction between the secular and the spiritual would have come naturally to them. We remember that Arnold's Rugby had been a kind of commonwealth in miniature where – at least after 1831 - Headmaster and Chaplain had been one and the same and preparation for Confirmation was seen as central to the whole Rugby experience. [19] Perhaps Tait and his successors saw the Nation as a School writ large, where the same union of spiritual and secular were equally vital. There is also an underlying theological justification. In "Tait's Creed" we find heavy emphasis on Original Sin and "the consequent impossibility of man being justified …" while Arnold often declared that evil was especially acute in "a society formed exclusively of boys, that is of elements separately weak and imperfect, becomes more than an aggregate of their several defects; the amount of evil in the mass is greater than the sum of evil in the individuals."[20] If England was only half as bad as Rugby, any separation of the spiritual and secular forces ranged against sin and iniquity could only play into the hands of evil. Indeed the doctrine of Original Sin was the key to the traditional Christian understanding of the purpose of the state. No state had

---

[17] *Church of the Future,* p. 13.
[18] *Ibid.*
[19] J. R. de S Honey *Tom Brown's Universe: the Development of the Victorian Public School,* London 1977, p. 5.
[20] Honey *op cit* p. 6.

been needed when Adam and Eve were still in Innocence but, once sin and death entered the world, the human race would surely have destroyed itself before God's plans for mankind could unfold. Thus it was God, in His infinite wisdom and mercy, who devised the state to curb the worst excesses of human wickedness. Luther put it nicely, "Princes are God's hangmen."

Tait's commitment to Establishment is linked to his hostility to the Catholic tradition, revealed in such phrases as "the peculiar encroachments of the Roman see" and "the return to exploded superstition." On a visit to a church in Perugia in 1845, he had been horrified by the spectacle of a naked man beating himself with iron chains, while the crowd "treated him with the respect paid to a dervish."

> It is from such scenes as these, not from the elegant Monsignori of Rome, that we must judge the evils of Rome. The scene was indeed like the worship of some heathen deity. This is surely Anti-Christ. And this is the city of an archbishop, and within the Pope's own territory.[21]

In *The Church of Future,* all chance of co-operation with Rome is ruled out:

> The Roman Catholic Church, indeed separates itself from us by so sharp a line of arrogant exclusiveness, built on a superstructure of false doctrine, that our hopes of influencing it must be very slight unless some fundamental change be made to its whole system.[22]

It is true that Tait calls his first Chapter, "The Church of the Future: its Catholicity" and calls for closer links with other churches. But the basis for such links is common hostility to Rome, with "Lambeth" (Tait himself) playing the leading role:

> Every year Lambeth is becoming more and more a centre to which the whole Anglican communion directly looks; and that communion seems to me more and more every year becoming itself a centre of

---

[21] Davidson and Benham, *Life of Tait, op cit,* vol.1, p 125.
[22] *Church of the Future,* p. 8.

all the Churches of Christendom which protest against Roman usurpation. [23]

He is only marginally less critical of the Catholic tradition within the Church of England. After a few words of faint praise for "what is commonly called the Oxford revival," he insists:

> Still I think it may be granted on the other hand – that the teaching thus introduced or resuscitated, notwithstanding all its claims to Catholicity, was and is based on a somewhat narrow system, and has confined Churchmen's sympathies in the direction in which before they were ready to expand. [24]

Of all Tait's actions as Archbishop, his most controversial role must be the passing of the Public Worship Act of 1874 - in which Parliament (already containing many non-Anglicans) ruled that the use of certain aspects of Catholic ceremonial in Anglican services was a criminal offence, punishable by imprisonment. This is a sensitive issue for Tait who devotes several pages of *The Church of the Future* to a defence of the measure:

> It is commonly said that that the Public Worship Regulation Act has altogether failed of its purpose. I must be allowed, as its chief promoter, to say that this is not so. Those who make such a statement do not rightly apprehend what its purpose was. Its promoters never desired that it should produce a crop of convictions and of punishments inflicted on wrong-headed conscientious men. What they desired was to put a stop to a state of things – common and growing six years ago – by which every raw theologian, visiting Belgium or some other neighbouring Roman Catholic country, came back laden with a crop of very doubtful innovations, which he sought to introduce into his own parish as an improvement on the authorised mode of worship, to the great annoyance and scandal of his sober-minded parishioners.[25]

Tait sees the Act as fulfilling his commitment to "maintaining the old Sacraments and the old ordinances and forms." Without the Act and without

---

[23] *Church of the Future*, p. 2.
[24] *Church of the Future*, p. 16.
[25] *Church of the Future*, pp. 20-21.

Tait's influence (strongly supported by the Queen) in securing the appointment of – mostly – Low- and Broad-Church Bishops, the Church of England would have moved several notches in the Catholic direction. Significantly, this was the trend in Provinces where the Anglican Church was not Established – hence the cry:

> With dark benighted faces,
> The Heathen ask us why,
> The Church in foreign places
> Should be so very High.

Tait's analysis is circular. He wants to keep Parliament in control because, left to its own devices, the Church might move too far in the direction of Ritualism, but he also wants to curb Ritualism because failure to do so will increase the danger of Disestablishment. He defends the Public Worship Act because it corresponds both to the voice of the nation, tested in Parliament, and to the voice of the Church. Ritualism is a clerical movement, disliked by the majority of the laity – who support the Act because it recognises "their right to be heard in matters concerning the common worship of their parish churches."[26] They want a "well ordered, hearty and attractive ritual, but are perfectly staunch in their dislike of semi-Romish innovations."[27] If Tait is right, the unchecked advance of Ritualism would so scandalise "sober-minded parishioners" that they might desert the Church altogether – either for other Churches or for unbelief – and that will be reflected in more support for Disestablishment in Parliament and in the country.

Tait is at least as concerned about the effects of Ritualism on relations with other Churches, especially Protestant Churches. He stresses long-standing ties with Calvinist Churches on the Continent:

> Neither are we forgetful how, in the persecution under Mary Tudor, our true-hearted Reformers found a refuge in Switzerland till the tyranny was over past, nor how there has ever been, since those days, a bond of cordial union, independent of outward forms, uniting the wisest spirits of the Church of England with the literary and theological labours of German, French and Swiss Protestants … The

---

[26] *Church of the Future*, p. 23.
[27] *Church of the Future*, p. 29.

boundaries of separation, then, between us and Continental Protestants who hold fast by the fundamentals of the Gospels, fade to an indistinct line.[28]

Significantly, the words "Apostolic Succession" – for those in the Catholic tradition precisely what makes the line distinct - do not appear once in the pages of *The Church of the Future*. Tait fears that "it will be our fault if the great Protestant communities throughout the world, which adhere to the apostolic faith, do not feel that their cause is indissolubly united with ours." [29] The "fault" can only be to allow the Church of England to move Rome-wards.

Tait's other controversial measure was the Burials Act of 1880, – upsetting many High Churchmen because it allowed Ministers of other Christian denominations (though not non-Christians) to hold funeral services in Anglican churchyards. Tait acknowledges that the Act is intended "to have something of a healing effect in reference to the general relations of Churchmen and Nonconformists." [30] *The Church of the Future* is friendly to Dissent:

> It is impossible to have a near union of worship and teaching with those who altogether repudiate our forms of prayer and of Church government, and look upon many of the statements made by our Church as superstitious and ungodly. But not the less it is our duty, where we can, to cultivate friendly relations with them, and draw them to us , by the manifestation of a real Christian spirit, while we look for occasions on which, notwithstanding out differences, we may act together for the spiritual good of the nation. [31]

The crucial point is that:

> For myself, in the office which in the providence of God, I have held now for nearly twelve years, I have certainly never experienced any unwillingness, on the part of our countrymen without our pale, to pay to the Church of England that deference which all Protestant

---

[28] *Church of the Future*, pp. 12-3.
[29] *Ibid.*
[30] *Church of the Future*, p.17.
[31] *Church of the Future*, p.14.

Christendom awards it, as the chief bulwark of the reformed faith against the assaults, on the one side, of superstition, and, on the other, of an aggressive infidelity.[32]

There are hints that Dissenters would not – or at least should not – object to the Established Church that provides a bulwark against superstition. Yet if the Church embraces superstition, why should they accept an Establishment that still discriminates against them? Perhaps Tait is right. It is hard to see how an overwhelmingly Anglo-Catholic Church could have remained Established. The fact of the Reformation could not have been erased. While some High Churchmen would have been glad to rid themselves of the constraints of Establishment, today there is a greater need than ever for an Established Church – to which most people do not belong but still feel somehow attached – to resist the advance of secularism.

But Tait's argument seems incomplete. If it makes sense not to permit further steps in the Catholic direction, would it not be better still for the Church to root out the remnants of Popery in its liturgy and doctrine – most of which were probably either objectionable or unintelligible to Tait's "sober-minded parishioners."? If the Church becomes more "doctrine-lite", Dissenters will surely queue up to join. There can then be a truly national Church with only a few extremists – Quakers, Unitarians and Papists – remaining outside the enlarged "pale." What is needed is Comprehension, not more toleration. This is surely the logic of Tait's analysis and was precisely the course that had been advocated by Tillotson and Arnold. "Tait's Creed" does talk of freeing the Church "from certain modern accretions on the one side or the other." But Tait is remarkably vague about what "accretions" should go.

Tait's hostility to "Superstition" is genuine but, contrary to the usual view, it is not his greatest concern. This is clear from the whole balance of *The Church of the Future*, where about half of the book is devoted to conflict with various forms of Infidelity. Tait is surely right to believe that, whereas in the past, debate has centred on what particular form of Christianity is most acceptable to God, the debate of the future will probably be about whether there is any God at all. Many questions, about which Christians might differ,

---

[32] *Church of the Future*, p. 19.

can wait "till formidable dangers, threatening the whole Church, are overpast."[33] The most striking passage in the entire book reads:

> Superstition may for a time raise its head, and does raise it in a strange and unexpected fashion in some of the countries of Europe, attracting numbers as if it were the only antidote to infidelity, instead of being, as I believe it is, the handmaid of the same evil influence. Men will never be cured of believing too little by unscrupulous attempts to involve them in believing too much ... It is well to note in history how these two evils, superstition and infidelity, act and react in strengthening each other. Still, I cannot doubt that the most formidable of the two for us at present is infidelity.[34]

Tait is confident that the Church can defeat the challenges of Atheism and Deism, because both are essentially "two very old forms of error" and can thus be refuted by "the approved old arguments." A bigger danger lies in Rationalism, especially in a nominally Christian rationalism:

> Presenting itself under the guise of an improved and more rational Christianity, speaking with greatest respect of the Lord Jesus Christ and His Apostles; professing to regard them as great benefactors of the human race, and even admitting that the historical Christ is in some sense a wonderful manifestation of God brought near to man, it virtually substitutes a new in the place of the old genuine Gospel ... Should it prevail, I fear we must bid farewell to a true conception of human nature and the hatefulness of sin, and lose the most powerful motives which can guide human life, and be content to sink to views of Christian duty and the elevation of the Christian character very different from those which animated the Apostles. [35]

Tait fears that the "cavilling of what calls itself the advanced criticism" may lead to a Christianity from which the supernatural element, even belief in the Resurrection, has been eliminated, and hence becomes "no Christianity at all."[36] In view of Tait's attitude to the Catholic tradition, it comes as a surprise to read, "I have great fear lest, in the long run, the faith

---

[33] *Church of the Future,* p. 33.
[34] *Church of the Future,* pp. 34-5.
[35] *Church of the Future,* pp. 90-1.
[36] *Church of the Future,* p. 92.

of our Church and country may suffer far more by abstraction from than by addition to its approved system of Christian doctrine."[37]

But how to get the balance right? There is undoubtedly a ghost in *The Church of the Future*. Tait is writing nearly forty years after he moved from Balliol to Rugby yet, as he approaches his own death, his thoughts turn to the last days of his predecessor:

> It has been noted also that the latter sermons preached by Dr. Arnold, before he was prematurely taken from the Church on earth in his forty-seventh year, to the sorrow of all good men, are marked by an earnest clinging to the great central doctrines of Christianity, and a vivid inculcation of them in their fullness on the souls of those for whose spiritual good he yearned. He was a man fearless in speculation, and had known many harassing doubts; but the deepening experience of a devout life and the ripening conviction of the realities of that eternal world which, though imperceptibly, he was nearing, had on his noble spirit that same effects which life's trials and the felt nearness of God may be expected to produce on all the most earnest truth-loving souls.[38]

It is the most moving and perceptive passage in *The Church of the Future* and reveals the importance of Arnold and – hence of Rugby – to Tait as a man and as a thinker. He was indeed a worthy successor to Arnold.

---

[37] *Church of the Future,* p. 89.
[38] *Church of the Future,* pp. 137-8.

Arthur Hugh Clough and Agnosticism

Anthony Kenny

In the latter part of the nineteenth century it was not uncommon to canonize, as the great poets of the Victorian age, a quartet whose members were Tennyson, Browning, Matthew Arnold and Arthur Hugh Clough. The reputation of the first three endured, but at the end of the century Clough was expelled from the pantheon. In the first half of the twentieth century Lytton Strachey sniggered at Clough's association with Florence Nightingale, and F.R. Leavis exalted the talents of Gerard Manley Hopkins above all four of the original Victorian quartet.

In 1941 Winston Churchill, anxious to secure American co-operation in the fight with Hitler, broadcast some lines from "Say not the struggle naught availeth" which ended "Westward, look, the land is bright". This brought some at least of Clough's poetry back to the national consciousness, and in the post-war years several critics were willing to hail him as the most modern of Victorian poets. Changing fashions in English departments in universities have led, since 1980, to comparative neglect of Clough's oeuvre, though popular editions of the principal poems have continued to appear regularly. The 150th anniversary of his death passed last year without any celebration of his memory other than the attachment of a blue plaque to his house in Camden Town.

However, Clough has retained a place in the history of nineteenth century England as a paradigm of religious doubt and disbelief. The Victorian Church of England produced a fine crop of doubters – whether they were interdenominational doubters such as John Henry Newman and Gerard Manley Hopkins, or post-Christian doubters like Matthew Arnold and Henry Sidgwick. But perhaps none of these, in their departure from Anglicanism, suffered such internal turmoil, or paid so heavy a worldly price, as did Clough. And certainly none gave such eloquent poetic expression to their internal religious struggle.

Clough entered Rugby in 1829, at the age of ten. His family lived in South Carolina and so during the vacations he was frequently entertained in the private residences of the headmaster, Thomas Arnold. There he struck up friendships which were to last a lifetime with the headmaster's sons Matthew and Tom. His schoolboy letters show great piety, and when he left Rugby for Balliol in 1837 he saw his future career in the church. "I have looked forward so long so continually to God's service, to a parish and its duties that they seem fixed as destiny could make them."

Oxford, however, quickly unsettled the earnest pieties he had learned at Arnold's feet. The University was in a state of religious turmoil caused by the new and growing Tractarian movement, whose most celebrated figure was John Henry Newman. Sacramental, doctrinaire Tractarianism was at the opposite extreme from the liberal Anglicanism of Thomas Arnold which was less concerned with the dogmatic formulation of religious truth and saw morality as the essence of Christianity.

Clough was quickly swept up in the Oxford debate, and, encouraged by his tutor W.G. Ward, he attended Newman's sermons and imitated Tractarian austerities. It was hard for him to reconcile his new Tractarian fervour with his continued devotion to Arnold, though for a while he believed that Newman had blest him with new wisdom. "How strange" he told himself "that I should owe so much to Arnold and so much to him! How have I deserved this second enlightenment?"

The poems of Clough's Balliol years display a profound sense of sin, of wasted effort and of duties unfulfilled. But his diaries of those years reveal also a gradual weakening of the Tractarian influence. In November 1838 he wrote of "the impolicy and sin of Athanasianism", by which he meant the thesis that human beings, if they hold the wrong doctrines, are damned in hell for ever, as proclaimed in the Athanasian creed. When the college syllabus obliged him to study the thirty-nine articles of the Church of England, he noted in his diary that he was visited with "dreadful feelings of unbelief and atheism".

In 1842, after a disappointing second class in Schools and a failure to obtain a Balliol Fellowship, Clough became a Fellow of Oriel, Newman's College. Despite occasional long discussions with his august new colleague, Clough was by now quite freed from the Tractarian spell. In 1843 his disenchantment went further: he began to chafe at the constraints imposed by any and every form of Anglicanism. To a friend in Tasmania he wrote:

> I have a very large amount of objection or rather repugnance to sign "ex animo" the 39 articles.... It is not so much from any definite objection to this or that point as general dislike to Subscription and strong feeling of its being... a bondage, and a very heavy one, and one that may cramp one and cripple one for life.

However, he overcame his scruples, in order to proceed to his M.A. and subscribed to the Articles.

A year later, his doubts returned, as recorded in a later letter to the same friend...

> If I begin to think about God, there arise a thousand questions, and whether the 39 articles answer them at all or whether I should not answer them in the most diametrically opposite purport is a matter of great doubt... Without the least denying Christianity I feel little that I can call its power. Believing myself to be in my unconscious creed in some shape or other an adherent to its doctrines I keep within its pale: still whether the spirit of the Age, whose lacquey and flunkey I submit to be, will prove to be this kind or that kind I can't the least say. Sometimes I have doubts whether it won't turn out to be no Christianity at all.

Soon after, Clough was forced to think once more about the constraints exercised by the thirty nine articles. W.G. Ward had moved further Romeward since the days when the two had been close at Balliol. In 1844 he published *The Ideal of a Christian Church* which argued that the Church of England was further from the ideal than the Church of Rome. The book was condemned by the University authorities as inconsistent with the articles and with Ward's good faith in signing them. Ward resigned his tutorship and was deprived of his degrees. A few months later Newman was received into the Roman Catholic Church.

Like Newman and Ward, Clough was now considering seceding from Oxford on religious grounds; but his doubts about the Church of England had quite different roots. Along with the Arnold brothers, he was now immersed in the disquieting works of authors such as George Sand, R.W. Emerson and Thomas Carlyle. Christianity no longer seemed to these old Rugbeians the sure refuge that it had always been to Dr Arnold senior. Matthew Arnold seems to have sloughed off Christian belief swiftly without any personal anguish; but Clough underwent slow stages of detachment.

A poem of 1845 addresses the confrontation between materialism and religion. It describes how mankind in its infancy had chased idols and false gods. Moses, in the dark cloud on Sinai, had brought the revelation of the one True God who spoke out of thunder.

> God spake it out, "I,God,am One";

> The unheeding ages ran
> And baby-thoughts again, again
>   Have dogged the growing man;
> And as of old from Sinai's top
>   God said that God is One,
> By Science strict so speaks he now
>   To tell us there is None!
> Earth goes by chemic forces; Heaven's
>   A Mécanique Celeste
> And heart and mind of human kind
>   A watch-work as the rest!

This new teaching, the poet tells us, is not to be compared with the voice of God: it is just a darkness concealing for a while a deeper truth that is yet to be revealed.

> 'Tis but the cloudy darkness dense;
>   Though blank the tale it tells,
> No God, no Truth! yet He, in sooth,
>   Is there – within it dwells;
> Within the sceptic darkness deep
>   He dwells that none may see
> Till idol forms and idol thoughts
>   Have passed and ceased to be.

The moral of the poem is that one should neither relapse, like the Puseyites, into the infantile idolatry of the Golden Calf, nor accept the current atheism of science as the last word from the mystic mountain Mankind should neither reject science, nor embrace superstition, but wait in faith for God to complete his plan of revelation.

The New Sinai, as the poem was entitled, presents a more coherent form of the interim Christianity which Clough had earlier held out as the justification for remaining an Oxford Anglican. But he continued to be uncomfortable, and contemplated resigning his tutorship. He was for a while attracted by Unitarianism, as represented in his home town of Liverpool by James Martineau. He speculated that he might find the irreligious university of London an environment more congenial to Christian belief. In Oxford, he complained "what religion I have I cannot distinguish from the amalgamations it is liable to." (M 141)

The year 1847 brought to a head the crisis in Clough's religious belief. He was impressed by the writings of the Tübingen school of criticism, especially of J.C. Baur and of D.F. Strauss, which questioned the historicity of the Gospels. Strauss's Life of Jesus, translated by George Eliot in 1846, rejected all the miraculous and supernatural elements in the Gospels, and regarded the presentation of Christ by the evangelists as the product of a collective myth.

Clough regarded the arguments of the Tübingen school as unanswerable, and to his sister he wrote that it the only thinker who helped him to continue in Christian belief was Coleridge. But he added:

> My own feeling certainly does not go along with Coleridge's in attributing any special virtue to the facts of the Gospel History….. I cannot feel sure that a man may not have all that is important in Christianity even if he does not so much as know that Jesus of Nazareth existed… Trust in God's Justice and Love, and belief in his Commands as written in our Conscience, stand unshaken, though Matthew, Mark, Luke and John, or even St Paul, were to fall.

These sentiments found expression in a verse entitled Epi-strauss-ion.

> Matthew and Mark and Luke and holy John
> Evanished all and gone!
> Yea, he that erst, his dusky curtains quitting,
> Through Eastern pictured panes his level beams transmitting
> With gorgeous portraits blent,
> On them his glories intercepted spent,
> Southwestering now, through windows plainly glassed,
> On the inside face his radiance keen hath cast,
> And in the lustre lost, invisible and gone,
> Are, say you, Matthew Mark and Luke and holy John
> Lost is it? lost to be recovered never?
> However,
> The place of worship the meantime with light
> Is, if less richly, more sincerely bright,

And in blue skies the Orb is manifest to sight.

The poem operates at several levels. The title Epi-Strauss-ion is modelled on two Greek words: epitaphion or epitaph and epithalamion or epithalamium. The poem is both an epitaph for the evanished evangelists, and an epithalamium for the wedding of divine wisdom and human scholarship. The allusion is to Psalm 19, which compares the divine law to the sun God has set in the sky. The central image is plain. The morning sun shines through the stained glass images in the chancel, the afternoon sun, shining through the plain windows of the nave, illuminates the church more brightly but less gorgeously as it deadens the images in the coloured glass. Just so, the legendary gospels are more colourful but less illuminating than the austere message of contemporary criticism. But the new learning enables the worshippers not only to see the world more clearly, but to have a less fractured vision of the source of light in God himself.

Clough's doubts about historical Christianity were combined with a profound theistic piety, expressed at this time in a poem entitled *Qui Laborat, Orat*. The first stanza is an invocation:

> O only source of all our light and life.
> Whom as our truth, our strength, we see and feel,
> But whom the hours of mortal moral strife
> Alone aright reveal!

The next three verses develop the theme that even the most abstract thoughts about God fall blasphemously short of the reality. Then come the crucial stanzas:

> O not unowned, Thou shalt unnamed forgive,
> In worldly walks the prayerless heart prepare,
> And if in work its life it seem to live
> Shalt make that work be prayer.
>
> Nor times shall lack, when, while the work it plies,
> Unsummoned powers the blinding film shall part,
> And scarce by happy tears made dim, the eyes
> In recognition start.

In December 1847 Clough told the Provost of Oriel that he no longer felt able to teach the thirty-nine articles, and in the following month he resigned his tutorship and went abroad.

1848 was a year of revolution throughout Europe. "Citoyen Clough" spent the spring in Paris, witnessing the French revolution at first-hand. Emerson was there too, and the two saw each other daily during May and June. When Emerson left Liverpool for America in July, Clough saw him off. He lamented his departure: Carlyle, he complained, had led everyone out into the desert and left them there. Emerson, in reply, laid his hand on Clough's head, and told him he was to be bishop of all England.

Clough's next act, however, took both his Anglican and his Emersonian friends by surprise. He spent the summer writing, not a religious tract, but a long narrative poem *The Bothie* about a reading party in Scotland. The poem was published in November: in the previous month Clough had finally resigned his Oriel fellowship. Soon followed a further publication, a collection entitled Ambarvalia which gave to the world *The New Sinai* and *Qui Laborat, Orat*.

From April to August 1849, Clough was in Rome where, since the expulsion of Pius IX in 1848, Mazzini had presided over a short-lived Roman Republic. Clough's letters give a vivid account of Garibaldi's defence of the city against the besieging French army under General Oudinot. With astonishing speed he exploited this experience in poetical form, writing an epistolary novel in five cantos, *Amours de Voyage*.

In October of the same year Clough became the head of University Hall, London, a non-sectarian collegiate institution for students attending lectures at University College. He was not happy there, finding it no easier to accommodate himself to the principles of the Unitarians and Presbyterians who governed it than to the articles of the Church of England which had troubled him at Oriel.

While in Rome, Clough had attended services conducted by the Anglican chaplain, Mr Hamilton, in a room outside the Porta del Popolo. But he had now for some time ceased to be a Christian believer. During August in Naples he gave poetic expression to his disbelief in the central Christian doctrine, the Resurrection of Christ. *Easter Day* passionately denies the

Resurrection, using the very words in which it is proclaimed in the Gospels and by St Paul.

> Christ is not risen, no
> He lies and moulders low,
>   Christ is not risen.
>
> What though the stone were rolled away, and though
>   The grave found empty there –
>   If not there, then elsewhere;
> If not where Joseph laid him first, why then
>   Where other men
> Translaid Him after; in some humbler clay
>   Long ere today
> Corruption that sad perfect work hath done,
> Which here she scarcely, lightly had begun.
>   The foul engendered worm
> Feeds on the flesh of the life-giving form
> Of our most Holy and Anointed one.
>
> He is not risen, no
> He lies and moulders low;
>   Christ is not risen.
>
> Ashes to ashes, dust to dust;
> As of the unjust, also of the just –
>   Christ is not risen.

The poem sets out, in terms as concrete as possible, what is involved in denying the Resurrection. It states alternative accounts to explain the Gospel stories, and draws out the consequences of each. If Jesus did not die, then his body has long since rotted. If the tomb was empty, as the Gospels says, that can mean only that Jesus' body had been moved elsewhere. The words of the burial service apply to Jesus, just as to any other human saint or sinner. Perhaps there were indeed appearances of Jesus to disciples after his death; but this need not mean a genuine rising from the dead.

St Paul told the Corinthians that if Christ was not risen from the dead, then they too would not rise. "If in this life only we have hope in Christ, we are of all men most miserable". Clough accepts Paul's conclusion as a truth, not a reductio ad absurdum.

>   Eat, drink, and die, for we are men deceived,
>   Of all the creatures under heaven's wide cope
>   We are most hopeless who had once most hope
>   We are most wretched that had most believed
>   Christ is not risen!
>
> Eat, drink, and play, and think that this is bliss!
>   There is no heaven but this!
>   There is no Hell;
> Save Earth, which serves the purpose doubly well,
>   Seeing it visits still
> With equallest apportionments of ill
> Both good and bad alike, and brings to one same dust
>   The unjust and the just
>   With Christ, who is not risen. (P. 201)

Easter Day is one of the most powerful of Clough's poems on religion. It speaks to believers and unbelievers alike. It speaks to, and for, unbelievers because of its unqualified and unblinking denial of the Resurrection. It speaks to believers because it accepts the importance of what is denied, and accepts unflinchingly that one who abandons Christianity has much to lose. The poem's compelling power derives from the skill with which the poet uses the language of the New Testament to negate the New Testament's key message.

Clough went on to write a poem entitled "Easter Day II", which proclaims "In the true Creed / He is yet risen indeed / Christ is yet risen" But it is clear that the kind of resurrection affirmed in this second poem is not a literal one, but one compatible with Jesus being, and remaining, dead. The poem – much less powerful than Easter Day itself – is not a reaffirmation of traditional Christianity, but simply a softening of the pessimism that accompanied its denial.

>   Now, too, as when it first began,

> Life is yet Life and Man is Man.
> For all that breathe beneath the heaven's high cope,
> Joy with grief mixed, with despondence hope.
> Hope conquers cowardice, joy grief:
> Or at the least, faith unbelief.
>> Though dead, not dead;
>> Not gone, though fled;
>> Not lost, not vanished
>> In the great Gospel and true Creed,
>> He is yet risen indeed;
>>> Christ is yet risen. (P.203)

Though much inferior as a poem to *Easter Day*, this sequel may well be a fairer reflection of Clough's own subsequent state of mind at this time. Later in the year he wrote one of the most devout of his poems *Hymnos Aumnos*. The first stanza invokes the incomprehensible Godhead

> O Thou whose image in the shrine
> Of human spirits dwells divine;
> Which from that precinct once conveyed
> To be to outer day displayed,
> Doth vanish, part, and leave behind
> Mere blank and void of empty mind,
> Which wilful fancy seeks in vain
> With casual shapes to fill again.

The initial assumption is that the place to look for God is in the individual's inmost soul. ("The Kingdom of God is within you"). Well and good; but attempts to give public expression to the God encountered in the soul yield only meaningless, self-contradictory utterances ("blank and void") or idle images with no contact with reality ("casual shapes").

After the second stanza of the poem has developed the theme of the impotence of human utterance to embody the divine, the third proclaims that silence – inner as well as outer – is the only response to the ineffable.

> O thou, in that mysterious shrine
> Enthroned, as we must say, divine!
> I will not frame one thought of what
> Thou mayest either be or not.

> I will not prate of "thus" and "so"
> And be profance with "yes" and "no".
> Enough that in our soul and heart
> Thou, whatso'er thou may'st be, art.

Clough's agnosticism, at this point, is radical. The *via negativa* is rejected as firmly as the *via positiva*. Not only can we not say of God what he is, we are equally impotent to say what he is not. The possibility, therefore, cannot be ruled out that one or other of the revelations claimed by others may after all be true.

> Unseen, secure in that high shrine
> Acknowledged present and divine
> I will not ask some upper air,
> Some future day, to place thee there;
> Nor say, nor yet deny, Such men
> Or women saw thee thus and then:
> Thy name was such, and there or here
> To him or her thou didst appear.

In the final stanza Clough pushes his agnosticism a stage further. Perhaps there is no way in which God dwells – even ineffably – as an object of the inner vision of the soul. Perhaps we could reconcile ourselves to the idea that God is not to be found at all by human minds. But even that does not take off all possibility of prayer.

> But only thou in that dim shrine,
> Unknown or known, remain, divine;
> There, or if not, at least in eyes
> That scan the fact that round them lies.
> The hand to sway, the judgement guide,
> In sight and sense, thyself divide:
> Be thou but there – in soul and heart,
> I will not ask to feel thou art. (P.312)

The soul reconciled to the truth that there can be no analogue of seeing or feeling God, that nothing can be meaningfully said about him, can yet – if Clough is right – address him and pray to be illuminated by his power and be the instrument of this action. To this day there has been no more eloquent attempt to be faithful to a critical agnosticism and yet draw support from the consolations of theism.

For the rest of his life Clough retained, with regard to religion, this stance of an agnosticism that made room for prayer. Perhaps it is not altogether correct to describe his position as agnostic: he seems always to have retained a belief in some kind of divinity, but undoubtedly the God he worshipped was an unknown God.

One of Clough's most often quoted – or misquoted - poems survives on a single undated sheet of paper. Entitled "The Latest Decalogue", it is a splendid piece of two-edged satire.

> Thou shalt have one God only; who
> Would be at the expense of two?
> No graven images may be
> Worshipped, except the currency.
> Swear not at all; for for thy curse
> Thine enemy is none the worse.
> At church on Sunday to atend
> Will serve to keep the world thy friend.
> Honour thy parents – that is, all
> From whom advancement may befall.
> Thou shalt not kill, but needs't not strive
> Officiously to keep alive;
> Do not adultery commit:
> Advantage rarely comes of it.
> Thou shalt not steal – an empty feat,
> When it's so lucrative to cheat.
> Bear not false witness; let the lie
> Have time on its own wings to fly.
> Thou shalt not covet, but tradition
> Approves all forms of competion.
>
> The sum of all is, thou shalt love,
> If any body, God above:
> At any rate shall never labour
> More than thyself to love thy neighbour. (P.205)

The most impressive verse embodiment of Clough's mature thought on religious topics is an unfinished dramatic poem, *Dipsychus*, which was begun on a visit to Venice in 1850. This is a Faust-like dialogue between a tormented youth, in two minds ("Dipsychus") about his future career, and a spirit (named in one version "Mephistopheles") who represents the temptations of the world, the flesh, and the devil. The dialogue is conducted in many different metres, from solemn quasi-Shakespearean blank verse to Gilbertian patter-songs. Here for the first time Clough raises not only worries about the doctrines of Christianity, but doubts about the very existence of God. Years before Nietzsche and Dostoievski he asks whether morality can survive the death of God.

> I dreamt a dream; till morning light
> A bell rang in my head all night
> Tinkling and tinkling first, and then
> Tolling; and tinkling; tolling again.
> So brisk and gay, and then so slow.
> O joy and terror! mirth and woe!
> Ting, ting, there is no God; ting, ting –
> Dong, there is no God; dong
> There is no God; dong, dong!
>
> Ting, ting, there is no God; ting ting;
> Come dance and play, and merrily sing –
> Ting, ting a ding, ting, ting a ding.
> O pretty girl who trippest along,
> Come to my bed – it isn't wrong.
> Uncork the bottle, sing the song.
> Come to my bosom, O my sweet.
> For guilt is nonsense, sin deceit
> Ere death end us, let us meet.
> Haven't we trembled long enough
> Because of that religious stuff?
> Come with the witty words and song
> And the rich liquor – come along
> My charmer – there's no right or wrong.
>
> Ting ting a ting: dong, dong
> Wine has dregs; the song an end

> A silly girl is a poor friend
> And age and weakness who shall mend?
> Dong, there is no God; Dong.
>
> O Rosalie, my precious maid
> I think thou thinkest love is true
> And on thy fragrant bosom laid
> I almost could believe it too.
> O, in our nook, unknown, unseen,
> We'll hold our fancy like a screen
> Us and the dreadful fact between
> And it shall yet be long, aye, long
> The quiet notes of our low song
> Shall keep us from that sad dong, dong.
> Hark, hark, hark! O voice of fear:
> It reaches us here, even here.
> Dong, there is no God; dong.

These stanzas may be set beside Matthew Arnold's well-known treatment of disbelief. *Dover Beach* offers, as the only consolation for the melancholy long withdrawal of faith, the bond between two lovers.

> Ah, love, let us be true
> To one another! for the world, which seems
> To lie before us like a land of dreams
> So various, so beautiful, so new
> Hath really neither joy, nor love, nor light
> Nor certitude, nor peace, nor help for pain…

The consolation surely fails: if in reality there is no such thing as love, what will keep the poet and his partner true to one another? Clough's treatment in *Dipsychus* is more consistent: love, too, without faith, is a delusion.

> Rosalie, my lovely maid,
> I think thou thinkest love is true;
> And on thy faithful bosom laid
> I almost could believe it true

> The villanies, the wrongs, the alarms
> Forget we in each other's arms
> No justice here, no God above;
> But where we are, is there not love ?
> What? What? thou also go'st? For how
> Should dead truth live in lover's vow?
> What, thou? Thou also lost? Dong
> Dong; there is no God; dong!

Dipsychus' dream is more consistent than Arnold's poem, but Arnold's pessimism is more complete than Clough's. For the final stanza of Dipsychus' musings weakens the effect of the whole by insisting that the sombre tolling of the bell of atheism is, after all, only a dream.

Having teased out the consequences of denial of God, Clough in the same drama analyses the motives of those who believe or disbelieve. The verses in which he does so, serious in purpose but light in execution, show him at his poetic best; and with them we may leave our consideration of his agnosticism.

> 'There is no God' the wicked saith
>   'And truly it's a blessing
> For what he might have done with us
>   It's better only guessing.'
>
> 'There is no God' a youngster thinks
>   'Or really if there may be
> He surely didn't mean a man
>   Always to be a baby.'
>
> 'There is no God, or if there is'
>   The tradesman thinks, 'twere funny
> If he should take it ill in me
>   To make a little money.'
>
> 'Whether there be,' the rich man says
>   'It matters very little,
> For I and mine, thank somebody,
>   Are not in want of victual.'

Some others, also, to themselves
    Who scarce so much as doubt it,
Think there is none, when they are well,
    And do not think about it.

But country folks who live beneath
    The shadow of the steeple;
The parson and the parson's wife,
    And mostly married people;

Youths green and happy in first love,
    So thankful for illusion;
And men caught out in what the world
    Calls guilt, in first confusion;

And almost every one when age,
    Disease, or sorrows strike him,
Inclines to think there is a God
    Or something very like Him.

William Temple: "Confident Living after Careful Prayer"[1]

David Urquhart

William Temple, Archbishop of Canterbury, Philosopher, Tutor, Headmaster, Priest, Bishop, Chairman, Broadcaster, is described as "the most significant Anglican churchman of the twentieth century." [2]

---

[1] Canon A.E. Baker Introduction to *Religious Experience* John Clarke 1958: 2.

A vigorous apologist for Christian faith, it was above all his fearless engagement with intractable economic and social issues that gave him national prominence. In short space we shall trace the roots of his beliefs and policies, account for his leadership in Church and Society and consider his continuing influence both for those of faith and none.

In the wide range of Temple's engagement in public life from 1908 to 1944 he faced issues still current today: the gap between universal education and persistent ignorance; confusion about family fragmentation and social cohesion; the uneasy relationship between Church and State; aspiring cooperation between Christian denominations; tension between social action and evangelism; the ethics of war and peace; dilemmas of poverty and wealth.

During a life of just over 63 years that "was always dominated by the immediate requirements of work" [3] Temple drew on a rich hinterland of classics, music, poetry, family, friendship and above all applied Christian theology.

William, the second son of Fredrick and Beatrice Temple, was born on 15th October 1881 in Exeter and educated at Rugby School, where his father had been Headmaster. At Balliol, Oxford, he followed his father with a double first.[4] Nurtured deeply in the 19th Century Establishment he sat lightly to inherited conventions. [5]

---

[2] www.justus.anglican.org. The author is grateful to Daniel Elphinston, St Andrew's University.

[3] Hastings Adrian *William Temple* Oxford Dictionary of National Biography.

[4] William and Fredrick are the only father and son to have both held the position of Archbishop of Canterbury. Edwards (1971: 286) best describes the similarity between William and his father; "William Temple was very much his father's son...both were self-confident and, while in theory they were democrats, in practice they relied little on the views of colleagues and cared even less about the attack of critics". On the other hand, William did not have his father's scientific knowledge or ability to exercise discipline over colleagues.

[5] In contrasting two successive Archbishops, Hastings writes "Lang was born humbly and cocooned himself with the trappings of high society; Temple was born to the purple and glad as Archbishop to open his own front door." History 1986: 255.

Temple "had a profound a profound veneration for both his parents".[6] His relationship with his father was both intellectual and affectionate, with a constant correspondence during his education, foreshadowing the days of email, "showing the intimate interchange of opinion, instruction and chaff". In his enthronement sermon of 1942, William said of his father "He was and is among men the chief inspiration of my life".[7]

Living with a cataract present from infancy that left him completely blind in his right eye, Temple possessed a near photographic memory that served him well, not only when preaching and lecturing, but also in reciting poetry and singing.

From student days he was a champion of Robert Browning, comparing him favourably to Shakespeare in a precocious undergraduate essay that stands the test of time:

"Shakespeare is magnificent but it is a pagan magnificence; Browning's genius is fundamentally and thoroughly Christian: through his poems there rings a joy of work and worship"[8]

Near the end of his life he wrote with wisdom that "The greatest literature is manifestly aiming at the presentation of a picture of human life in such ways that we may understand it more fully, not with a utilitarian aim, but because there is a joy in the understanding itself"[9]

Temple displayed from an early age that he was quick of mind and an intellect at heart. A persistent student on a quest for learning, he rose to Rugby sixth form at the earliest possible age, 15 ½. His relentless work ethic has been captured in one of the letters to his father:

"How could any intelligent boy who was able to get through two hours' work in thirty minutes spend the remaining ninety minutes

---

[6] (Baker 1946: 11-12).
[7] Temple W. *The Church Looks Forward* 1944: 5.
[8] Iremonger 1948: 47.
[9] Temple W. The *Resources and Influence of English Literature* (National Book Council London) 1943: 15.

except by adding to his store of knowledge" (Iremonger 1948: 16, 18)[10]

Temple continued in this vein at Oxford, graduating to a Fellowship at Queen's, in 1904. He was elected to an exhibition, his good humour and equanimity outweighing any hint of priggishness or pomposity.

Among the strongest influences at Balliol during Temple's time, followers of TH Green, Edward Caird promoted dialectical idealism on Hegelian lines while Cook Wilson moved steadily towards a realist philosophy.[11] Temple was an active member of the Union, holding positions as Secretary and Librarian in 1903 and President in the Lent Term of his last year. He spoke often, three times in a single week at the Union in his last year, finding no difficulty in developing a style that was at once confident in argument and sympathetic to opponents.

The study of Philosophy, and Plato in particular, that undergirded Temple's theological and religious development gave him a broad platform on which to build his understanding of God and the world. This interdisciplinary approach foreshadows the even wider base of the stimulating Philosophy of Science courses pioneered today by Rugby School.

Temple's two larger written works trace his journey towards a convinced Christian framework for life. In *Mens Creatrix* when discussing his assertion that "Pelagianism is Ethical Atheism", another good essay topic, his Liberal confidence in divine-human relationship emerges:

"At His own time He will call out from our hearts the response to His own love by the full manifestation of it in its irresistible power.

---

[10] Temple's biographer observes "The [Rugby] timetable exactly suited him (why it suited William Temple and disgusted R.G. Collingwood would make a good subject for an Upper Bench essay today)." (Iremonger 1948 : 16).

[11] Temple to the end proclaimed on numerous occasions the debt he owed to Caird as the greatest of all his teachers. Caird's influence on Temple went further than merely academic for Caird, in the many years prior to his move south, had come to know the "industrial progress of Glasgow with the horrible conditions under which thousands of the city's poor were forced to live". Caird pleaded for "improvement in the status of women in the factory, in the professions and at the ballot-box" (Iremonger 1948: 42).

So far as we have felt it, we prepare ourselves for a fuller response; so far as we trust those who tell us of it, we prepare ourselves to respond when the time will come." (Temple 1917: 290)

By the time of Christus Veritas he is developing his ideas of Christian engagement with society. From God's perspective:

"the whole purpose of human history is to fashion souls, and a great fellowship of the souls, knit together in mutual love through common participation in the Eternal love." (Temple 1924: 197)

About individual human conversion and the transformation of life Temple says:

"It is at once clear…that the thought of eternity is a most potent influence." (ibid: 207)

Daunting as these substantial essays are to the general reader, Michael Ramsey, theologian-bishop, and later a successor at both York and Canterbury, does not count Temple as a mainstream scholar. Nonetheless Ramsey concedes:

"… if Temple was the amateur he was yet, par excellence, the theologian. For him, everything was related to God, and to be cherished and studied in that revelation."[12]

As Temple entered public life, his theories were moulded and developed by active engagement, whether in the Student Christian Movement, the Workers Educational Association or later in the Coal and General Strikes of 1925 and 1926.[13] "His social concern was at the start an idealistic but shadowy socialism. He remained, however, all his life a man of tempered enthusiasm, resiliently skilful in grafting into his thinking new patterns of ideas."[14]

---

[12] Ramsey 1960: 147.
[13] In 1889, his father, Fredrick, was actively involved in the negotiations of the London Dock Strike. (Dark 1942).
[14] Hastings 1986: 300.

On neither extremes of Left or Right, a member of the Labour Party from 1918-1925, his methods can be followed up in the late RH Preston's extensive consideration of applied ethics, including the use of Middle Axioms.[15]

As the Dictators grew more powerful across Europe, Temple became more insistent that principles and their application are much more valuable than ideology. Articulating those principles in the Christian tradition is a hallmark of his achievement.

After 1928 Temple's ideas were developed further in the Henry Scott Holland Memorial Lectures, on Christianity and the State, and the Gifford Lectures of 1932-3. In the latter can be found his famous sentence "Christianity is the most avowedly materialistic of all the great religions".

In considering his motivation for public engagement in the Church and the World, it is important to realise that for Temple, as for many people of faith today, there is an integration of personal belief, action and reflection. The faithful life, therefore, is not simply a private matter, nor an easy choice, but an intentional outward response to the call to love God and neighbour.

Observing their practise of Christian religion, Ramsey compares nicely Temple's spirituality with that of Charles Gore, first Bishop of Birmingham (1905), who, like Temple, was passionate about Christianity and Society:

> "Gore, ever wearing the scars of doubt and conflict as to the love of God, but sure that the orthodox Creed with its miracles was the only one which made God and his love credible; Temple, serene in his faith in Christ, but searching long as to whether the orthodox understanding of that faith were the true one." [16]

It is sometimes argued that religion and belief should be separate from public life and leadership of the church and absolutely distinct from the theory and practise of organising and running a country or region. Temple

---

[15] Ronald H. Preston *The Future of Christian Ethics* SCM London 1987 ed R. John Elford and Ian S. Markham *The Middle Way* SCM London 2000. Middle Axioms are statements of policy which occupy the middle ground between specificity on the one hand and generality on the other. (Elford and Markham 2000:11).
[16] Ramsey 1960: 147.

was clear that it was no part of Christian activity to prescribe specific programmes or policies (that is the role of government) but it was an urgent Christian duty to articulate and live the principles by which those political decisions might be made. This imperative was not just for bishops and clergy but for all Christians, the vast majority of whom are lay people.

We can speculate tantalisingly on what Temple would have made of the pluralism with which the Church of England bishops work today where Christians in the West "are passing through a period of multiple endings"…and "the story of the gospel is lost in an act of collective amnesia." (Smith 2007: 23) David Smith looks out at contemporary uncertainty and sees a likely alliance between humanists, Muslims and Christians in seeking the Common Good. [17]

Certainly there is no shortage of public work for Lords Spiritual in England in 2012 whether in chairing the Hillsborough Enquiry, serving on the Parliamentary Banking Commission, or leading the Birmingham Social Inclusion Process. [18]

Temple, great man of the Church, like many effective priests, was not admitted for ordination without struggle. Though the dilemma, discernment and decision of a hundred years ago are familiar, the arrangements then are in stark contrast to the lengthy report writing, laborious interviewing and scientific analysis of today's recruitment in the Church of England. He had written to Francis Paget, Bishop of Oxford rather than starting on the privileged route via his father's successor at Lambeth, Archbishop Randall Davidson. Paget's reasoning for denying Temple ordination focussed on his 'shaky' beliefs and position regarding the Virgin Birth and the Resurrection. In response, Temple wrote to Davidson setting in motion a visit to Davidson at Lambeth and an exchange of letters between Davidson and Paget over a 2 year period concluding with Temple's ordination as priest on 19th December 1909.[19]

Long before he was ordained as a minister in the Church, Temple was a leader in education. As secretary, lecturer and eventually president (1908 –

---

[17] Smith David S. *Moving Towards Emmaus* (SPCK London) 2007: 8.
[18] The Bishops of Liverpool, Durham and the author, respectively.
[19] The exchange of letters between Davidson and Paget can be found in Iremonger 1948: 115-121.

1924) of the Workers Educational Association he had been influenced not just by his tutor, Caird, but by Albert Mansbridge, who founded the WEA in 1903 to "support the educational needs of working men and women who could not afford to access further or higher education" [20] The ideals that drew Temple to the WEA were shared by his friend RH Tawney:

> "Christian people should be concerned not only with that of the society of their personal lives but also with that of the society in which they lived". [21]

Temple's brief tenure as Headmaster of Repton was out flanked before and after by his life long commitment to adult education. Where and with whom is the current learning and discussion about our challenges and their proposed solutions? [22]

Temple and fellow Rugbeian Tawney were both influenced early by the then idealistic involvement of independent Public Schools in the slums of East London. This early insight that a well-rounded education includes personal experience of other cultures and classes is reflected today in some 'gap-year' activities and in the higher value put on volunteering and extra-mural commitments. Finding ways to turn these experiences into strategic, society-changing life is more elusive both with the uneven progress of Corporate Social Responsibility in powerful global capitalism and the deep-seated reluctance of able women and men to engage in political activity.

Countering a consumer culture, some citizens find satisfaction in socially cohesive charitable endeavour, for example through schools, personal and domestic care, sport or environmental stewardship. Will creative economic enterprise and less-selfish neighbourliness be enough to build a renewed, resilient, adaptable Britain where all can flourish?

Once Temple had moved to Manchester as Bishop he added rapidly to his understanding of and action for the disadvantaged. In the midst of reorganising a diocese of over 3.5 million people, by creating the Diocese of

---

[20] www.wea.org.uk.
[21] Ibid.
[22] Who is discussing for example: Jesse Norman's *The Big Society*, David Willett's *The Pinch*, Robert Skidelsky's *Keynes*, Richard Wilkinson and Kate Pickett's *The Spirit Level*, Jonathan Sacks *The Home We Build Together* or Miroslav Wolf's *A Public Faith*?

Blackburn for Lancashire, he also chaired a pivotal Conference on Christian Politics, Economics and Citizenship (COPEC) that met in Birmingham in 1924. With an introductory thought, familiar 90 years on, that "Machiavellian statecraft is bankrupt" (Iremonger 1948: 335) the conference aimed to "integrate Christian Faith and contemporary social responsibility" (ibid).

That intention came into focus again in wartime with the substantial papers (by inter al PTR Kirk, DM McKinnon and Dorothy Sayers) written for the 1941 Malvern Conference on Social Order and in the popular Penguin publication of Temple's, *Christianity and Social Order* (1942). The latter describes the Church's proper role, discusses Natural Order and illustrates three principles of the family as the primary social unit, the sanctity of personality and fellowship. If it be thought that the Church, in a purist understanding of Temple, was not permitted to make practical suggestions, then the list of six objectives on pages 73-74 of the pamphlet, for children, housing, leisure and liberty is both refreshing and useful in sharpening our priorities today.

Temple's understanding that society is more than the state and has a life which is largely independent of the state and that there is an inter-relationship, in his terms, between Community, State and Association, helps to navigate today's imbalance between national and local power and the appropriate use of scarce resources. [23]

In a surprising illustration of this inter-dependence, the current Coalition Department of Communities and Local Government approached the Church of England in 2011 to create and support the Church Urban Fund Near Neighbours initiative for developing cross-cultural inter-faith friendships in the inner cities of Bradford, Birmingham, Leicester and London.[24]

Within the Church, extensive efforts in ecumenical unity were more engaging and fruitful for Temple than the rather understated work of the Doctrine Commission of the Church of England which met sporadically from 1923 to 1938.

---

[23] Temple W. *Christianity and the State* 1928: 103.
[24] www.faithfulneighbourhoods.org.uk.

From the Edinburgh International Missionary Conference in 1910, through the Lausanne Conference on Faith and Order 1927 to the Life and Work Conference held at Utrecht in 1938, Temple attended, addressed, drafted and chaired the movements amongst protestant denominations that lead to the post second world war World Council of Churches:

> after Lausanne "The two main points on which the Conference was agreed were that the Faith of the Church is that to which the Apostles' and Nicene Creeds bear witness and that if unity of Order is to be achieved, it must rest on the basis of the historic episcopate." (Iremonger 1948: 401)

Of course the Church is seldom without internal controversy. The Faith and Order movement came under intense criticism, with the Bishop of Gloucester writing to Temple:

> "You are practically destroying the Faith and Order Movement…and very probably destroying a great deal of the Re-union movement" (Iremonger 1948: 412)

Temple was instrumental in the creation of the British Council of Churches which was to represent the British arm of the World Council. Of all Temple's achievements with this movement, the most outstanding and noteworthy is that Temple was nominated alone to lead the new advance.[25]

Nor did he neglect relations with the Orthodox and Roman Catholic Churches. Towards the ends of his life, Temple had plans to make a personal approach to the Vatican in the hope Anglican and Catholic theologians might undertake joint study of Natural Law as the basis of Christian Living.

To corral Temple narrowly as a social activist or church politician is to miss the point, not only of his solid personal faith but also of his passion that faith should be shared. One of his most attributed phrases today is that 'the

---

[25] "If the answer could be summarized in a sentence, it would be that all with whom Temple was associated knew that they could trust him as a thinker, as a chairman and as a friend. He was well grounded in the history of social, theological, and philosophical thought and, while remaining exactly sure of his own position, seemed to understand almost instinctively the traditions and tenets of other churches and other men" (Iremonger 1948: 415).

Church exists for those who are not its members'. Whether at missions on Blackpool sands, in the pulpits of Oxford University or broadcasting on the wireless, he proclaimed Jesus Christ as Lord.

In an address to clergy on Evangelism in our Time (Temple: The Hope 1940: V) he reflects on the challenges facing those preaching salvation, easily recognisable today. Whereas the sin of the world might be recognised, personal sin is an "alien concept". Education has been overwhelmed by the dominance of scientific "proof" and social order by the deterministic urge that immorality can be 'cured'. Nonetheless he argues that progress, a "20th C discovery" is not inevitable and that frustration is widespread. The struggles described in Romans chapter 7 reach across the ages.[26] With insight that critical viewers of TV soap operas (Eastenders and Hollyoaks come to mind) might find useful, Temple observes that human character is a fearful accumulation of evil, "generous, perhaps with superfluities but ruthlessly self-centred when our real or intimate interests are touched". (ibid: 109)

His most popular spiritual text was *Readings on John's Gospel*, an accessible pastoral support for a whole generation, where he writes, about Nicodemus' interview with Jesus by night: "the whole conception of the Kingdom is so novel that only those who are ready to make a new start can even see it, let alone enter into it." (Temple 1950: 49)

During Temple's time in Manchester he championed the cause of women, and the equalising ideas of the Board of Women's Work, as fellow human beings whose personalities God held sacred as part of the laity and of God's creation. This viewpoint was shared by his wife, whose spiritual zeal and practical work in this movement have often been regarded as critical to its success. With the 25th anniversary of the ordination of women deacons and historic votes on admitting women to the episcopate in 2012 we have moved on a long way from his empathetic reply to a correspondent on July 27 1943:

"…I am bound to add that I do not think the question of ordaining women to the priesthood in this country will become a live issue for a considerable time, if ever." [27]

---

[26] "For I do not do the good I want, but the evil I do not want is what I do" Romans 7:19 *Holy Bible* NRSV Collins 2007.
[27] Temple W. *Some Lambeth Letters 1942-1944* OUP 1963 No. 80.

Temple, despite disagreeing with their views, could show a sympathy and consideration towards pacifists that had not been known in the First World War. Much of the correspondence that he received protested against one form of bombing and fighting or another; but despite the extraordinary number of letters, each of Temple's responses were personal, reserving his anger only for those calling for reprisals against Germany. Temple was all too aware of the grief that losses caused by the War induced, but despite this he did not allow his sympathy to transgress the truth as he held it. During the Second World War he never neglected the armed forces and on several occasions he made personal visits.[28]

With his natural ease for broadcasting, the outbreak of hostilities in 1939 found Temple beginning his war-time addresses to the nation and beyond, first while Archbishop of York and then Canterbury. He had a clear understanding of his role. In his addresses; "Temple laid down for himself one standard – only for the *Christian* conscience could he or would he speak" (Iremonger 1948: 541). One such address from St Martin in the Fields in 1944 evoked such a reaction, that almost every European country sent messages of thanks for the inspiration and his prayers. "Now we understand what Christianity really is", wrote a soldier from overseas. (Iremonger 1948: 41)

Temple is read neither by those who give priority to rescuing individual souls in a fallen world nor by those who want new tools with which to engage in a global economy that has become plural and networked. Those who can recognise his huge range and dedicated contribution to building up Church and Society for nearly 40 years will appreciate his use and understanding of the now-favoured phrase 'social cohesion'.[29] In strengthening faith, family, church, trade and professional associations, businesses, voluntary movements, by the exercise of the principles of freedom, fellowship and service, all can flourish.

In a seminal critique of *Christianity and Social Order*, Malcolm Brown asks:

"Is dialogue with culture and a practice of 'public theology' remotely possible or is it a dangerous illusion which leeches Christian faith

---

[28] Temple became the first Archbishop to go to the battlefield since the Middle Ages when he visited troops in 1944 as part of Operation Overlord.
[29] Temple W. *Christianity and the State* 1928: 109.

and practice of all that is truly of God? One has only to reflect on the trials besetting Temple's successor at Canterbury, Rowan Williams, to conclude that something more than skilled chairing and elegant drafting are required to reconcile such divisions in the church today."[30]

The 105th Archbishop of Canterbury is being recruited against a list of at least six jobs in one: Bishop to the Canterbury Diocese; Metropolitan throughout the 30 dioceses of the Province of Canterbury; Primate of All England ('chaplain to the nation'); Focus of Unity for the world wide Anglican Communion; Ecumenical President; Inter-faith Leader. [31]

In one of William Temple's last addresses, to the Aquinas Society, he prophesied that when the war ends, "then multitudes will feel bewildered and lost; they will not know where they are, whither they are going nor even whither they wish to go. They will desperately need a map of the country." (Baker 1946: 230)

Even in wartime Temple could find time to address the Bank Officers' Guild on The Christian View of the Right Relationship between Finance, Production and Consumption,[32] an inspiring and courageous attempt at setting a new direction that might be emulated in the current financial crisis.

As religion, since 9/11, is a major element of public policy-making, and social inclusion processes identify the facts of personal loneliness, isolation and safety in a diverse population that faces stringent budget cuts and youth unemployment, with little trust in institutions or authority, the need for moral and spiritual guidance for persons and society is as great as ever.

Is the call of God who "so loved the world"[33] being heard for an Archbishop who, like William Temple, will show the Church how to reach out beyond herself "to proclaim the gospel afresh in each generation"[34]?

---

[30] (Brown: Journal of Anglican Studies :7).
[31] Crown Nominations Commission 2012.
[32] Temple W *The Church Looks Forward* 1944: 140.
[33] *Holy Bible* John 3:16.
[34] Preface to the Oaths and Declarations taken by those holding a bishop's licence.

William Temple Chronology

1881	Born on 15 October
1894	Rugby School
1900	Balliol, Oxford
1902	Father died
1904	Queen's College, Fellow and Lecturer in Philosophy Student Christian Movement
1904	Robert Browning essay
1905	Workers Educational Association (President 1908-24)
1908	Ordained Deacon aged 27 (Priest 1909)
1910	Headmaster of Repton aged 29
1914	Rector of St James, Piccadilly aged 33
1915	Mother died
1916	Married Frances Anson on 24 June
1917	*Mens Creatrix* published
1919	Canon of Westminster, Chair of Life and Liberty Movement
1921	Bishop of Manchester aged 39
1923	Doctrine Commission (reported 1938)
1924	*Christus Veritas* published Conference on Christian Politics, Economics and Citizenship (COPEC)
1927	Lausanne World Conference on Faith and Order
1928	Jerusalem National Missionary Council Prayer Book revision
1929	Archbishop of York aged 48
1930	Lambeth Conference
1932	Gifford Lecturer
1936	Lectures in United States of America
1942	Archbishop of Canterbury aged 61 Christianity and Social Order published
1944	Died on 26 October

Bibliography

Atherton et al. *Crucible* (Hymns Ancient and Modern: Oxon) Vol. 1, 2009
Baker A. E. (Cannon) *William Temple and His Message* (Penguin Books: London) 1946
Bentley Michael *The Life and Thought of Herbert Butterfield* (Cambridge University Press) 2011

Brown Malcolm *Poiltics as the Church's Business* (Journal of Anglican Studies vol 5(2): 163-186 SAGE) 2007
Dark S. *The People's Archbishop: The Man and His Message* (Rush and Warwick: Bedford)
Edwards D. L. *Leaders of the Church of England 1828-1944* (Oxford University Press: London) 1971
Grimley Mathew *Citizenship, Community and the Church: Liberal Anglican Theories of the State between the Wars* (Oxford University Press) 2004
Hastings Adrian *A History of English Christianity 1920-1985* (Collins: London) 1986
Higginbotham G. *Rugby School Register: Jan 1892 – Sep 1921* Vol. IV (Rugby: Rugby) 1929
http://en.wikipedia.org/wiki/William_Temple_(bishop) - (accessed 30/07/2012)
http://justus.anglican.org/resources/bio/61.html (accessed 30/07/2012)
http://www.spartacus.schoolnet.co.uk/REtempleW.htm (accessed 30/07/2012)
http://www.williamtemplefoundation.org.uk/ (accessed 30/07/2012)
http://www.answers.com/topic/william-temple-archbishop (accessed 30/07/2012)
Iremonger F.A. *"William Temple: Archbishop of Canterbury – His Life and Letters"* (Oxford University Press: London) 1948
Kent J. *William Temple: Church, State and Society in Britain, 1880-1950* (Cambridge University Press: Cambridge) 1992
Matthews W. R. et al *William Temple: An Estimate and An Appreciation* (Westminster Press: London) 1946
Palmer B. *A Class of Their Own: Six Public School Headmasters who became Archbishop of Canterbury* (The Book Guild: Sussex) 1997
Platten et. Al *Crucible* (Hymns Ancient and Modern: Oxon) Vol. 2 2009
Ramsey A. M. *From Gore to Temple: The Development of Anglican Theology between* Lux Mundi *and the Second World War 1889-1939* (The Hale Memorial Lectures at Seabury-Western Theological Seminary, 1959) (Longmans: London) 1960
Rugby School *The Meteor No. 897* 15/12/1944 (p95)
Smith David *Moving Towards Emmaus Hope in a Time of Uncertainty* (SPCK London) 2007
Temple W. *About Christ (The Archbishop's lectures in 1921 and 1925 on 'The University of Christ' and 'Christ's Revelation of God')* (SCM Press: London) 1962 (reprint)
Temple F. S. *William Temple: Some Lambeth Letters* (Oxford University Press: Oxford) 1963
Temple W. *A Conditional Justification of War* (Hazel, Watson & Viney: London) 1940
Temple W. *Christian Democracy* (Student Christian Movement Press: London) 1937
Temple W. *Christianity and Social Order* (Penguin Books: Middlesex) 1942
Temple W. *Christianity and The State* (Macmillan & Co: London) 1928
Temple W. *Christus Veritas* (Macmillan & Co: London) 1924
Temple W. *Citizen and Churchmen* (Eyre & Spottiswoode: London) 1941
Temple W. *The Church Looks Forward* (Macmillan & Co: London) 1944
Temple W. *Mens Creatrix* (Macmillan & Co: London) 1917

Temple W. *The Hope of a New World* (Student Christian Movement Press: London) 1940

Temple W. *The Nature of Personality: A Course of Lectures* (Macmillan & Co: London) 1911

Temple W. *Nature, Man and God* (The Gifford Lectures, University of Glasgow, 1932-1934) (Macmillan & Co: London) 1934

Temple W. *The Preacher's Theme To-Day (Four Lectures Delivered at the College of Preachers, Washington)* (Morehouse Publishing: London) 1936

Temple W. *Readings in St John's Gospel* (First and Second Series) (Macmillan & Co: London) 1950

Temple W. *Religious Experience (and other Essays and Addresses)* (James Clarke & Co: London) 1958

Temple W. *The Resources and Influence of English Literature* (Cambridge University Press: Cambridge) 1943

Warner H. C. *Daily Readings From William Temple* (Hodder & Stoughton: London) 1951

Matthew Arnold

Robin Le Poidevin

In 1984, the BBC broadcast a series of programmes written and presented by Don Cupitt, then an Anglican priest, Dean of Emmanuel College, Cambridge, and a controversial figure in religious debate. In these programmes, Cupitt unfolded a radical vision of a 'Christianity in change', one which was moving away from belief in an external, transcendent God, in favour of a personal commitment to a morally demanding way of life whose authority was wholly human. For the title of the series, Cupitt chose *The Sea of Faith,* a phrase from Matthew Arnold's best-known poem, 'Dover Beach'. This evocative metaphor was adopted by a movement—the Sea of Faith network—founded soon after the series, and in response to it, in which radical clergy and laity grouped together to explore, in a series of conferences and publications, the implications of the religious revolution described by Cupitt, but prefigured by Arnold.

'Dover Beach' paints a vivid picture of a moonlit scene, filled with the sounds of an ebbing tide. The Sea of Faith is going out, leaving the world bereft, and man confronting the blind forces of a godless universe:

> Listen! You hear the grating roar
> Of pebbles which the waves draw back, and fling,
> At their return, up the high strand,
> Begin and cease, and then again begin,
> With tremulous cadence slow, and bring
> The eternal note of sadness in…..
>
> The Sea of Faith
> Was once, too, at the full, and round earth's shore
> Lay like the folds of a bright girdle furl'd.
> But now I only hear
> Its melancholy, long, withdrawing roar,
> Retreating, to the breath
> Of the night-wind, down the vast edges drear
> And naked shingles of the world.
>
> Ah, love, let us be true
> To one another! for the world, which seems
> To lie before us like a land of dreams,
> So various, so beautiful, so new,
> Hath really neither joy, nor love, nor light,
> Nor certitude, nor peace, nor help for pain:
> And we are here as on a darkling plain
> Swept with confused alarms of struggle and fight,
> Where ignorant armies clash by night.[1]

---

[1] For this and other poems, see Allott (1965).

Those famous lines, and others in which Arnold portrays the grief, loss and longings of human existence, have earned him the reputation of a poet of pessimism. But contemporaries noted the contrast between the melancholy of his poems and the cheerfulness of his manner. And when he abandoned poetry in favour of critical writing his message was far more hopeful. Arnold was, beside a poet, an educationalist and critic, with a distinctively modern vision of the nature and purpose of human life. His conception of religion is as radical, and as positive, as that offered by Cupitt in 1984. But Arnold was writing in the 1870s, and so revolutionary was his message (though he was, in part, responding to currents of contemporary thought), that it was considered controversial, even dangerous, a century later.

So what was the path that led to Dover Beach and beyond?

Matthew Arnold was born on Christmas Eve, 1822, the second child and eldest son of Thomas and Mary Arnold. Matthew's father was not yet the celebrated Dr Arnold, Headmaster of Rugby, but at that time ran, in collaboration with William Buckland, a school in Laleham, near Staines in Middlesex. Until he was eight, Matthew was educated at home. But two years after Dr Arnold's appointment at Rugby, Matthew was sent back to Laleham to attend Buckland's school. It was not a great success—Matthew himself considered it a dismal institution—and he returned home in 1832 to be educated by a tutor. Finally, and with some reservations, his father decided to send both Matthew and his younger brother Tom to his old school, Winchester, recognising that they could not indefinitely be kept from the company of their peers, though fearing the corrupting influence of public school life. Brief though his time there was to be, Matthew managed to make himself rather unpopular at Winchester, as a result of remarking to the Headmaster, in front of a rather backward senior boy, that that he considered the work 'light and easy'. The remark was reported, and Matthew found himself being pelted with missiles from his outraged schoolfellows. After a year, Dr Arnold decided that evil was more rife at Winchester than at Rugby, and Matthew moved there in 1837.

Contemplating Dr Arnold's formidable reputation as a moral educator, we might suppose Matthew found him a remote and forbidding father, and that the gulf between father and son would have been widened still further by the fact that Matthew's father was also his headmaster. But, although the clear moral vision must often have been evident, relations between the two were genuinely warm. In letters Dr Arnold addresses Matthew as 'My dearest Matt', and both contributed humorous articles to a home-made periodical, the *Fox How Magazine*, named after their holiday retreat in the Lake District. In these, Dr Arnold would occasionally make gentle fun of Matthew, whom he nicknamed 'Crab' because of his awkward way of walking, as a result of a slight deformity of the legs (for which he was obliged to wear leg irons for a number of years).

At Rugby, Matthew appears, outwardly at least, not to have been too much in awe of his father. His manner was relaxed, even frivolous. He was late for school, and did not exert himself in his father's history lessons, even, according to one report, pulling faces when the headmaster's back was turned. Matthew's apparent lack of seriousness was a source of concern to his parents, and he must have often been compared unfavourably, as Prince Hal to Hotspur, with one of Arnold's star pupils, Arthur Hugh Clough. Clough had a brilliant career at Rugby, and was keenly aware of Arnold's Christian ideal of conduct, which he shared. He was a visitor and honorary family member at Fox How in the holidays. Later, at Oxford, Matthew and Clough were to develop a close friendship. But in those early days, Clough, who was Matthew's senior by three years, must have seemed something of an unwelcome model.

For the Arnold children, school holidays had never meant a complete break from schoolwork: exercises in Greek and Latin would be set and progress continually monitored. Towards the end of Matthew's time at Rugby, an Oxford Tutor, William Lake, was engaged to prepare Matthew for the Balliol Scholarship examination. After a summer of tuition, Lake reported to Dr Arnold in negative terms, and expectations of success were not high. Matthew nevertheless won a scholarship, and went up to Balliol in 1841. Here, he was able to foster his frivolity and foppishness in the typical manner of a nineteenth-century undergraduate, causing the Master of Balliol to judge him 'indolent'. He was very soon joined in Oxford by his father, who was appointed to the Regius Professorship of History in the same year. This coveted appointment Dr Arnold was not able to enjoy for long, however, as he suffered a series of seizures the following summer, and died in June, 1842, at the age of forty seven.

Matthew Arnold's feelings about his father were given public expression in his poem 'Rugby Chapel', written in 1857, when the poet was thirty-five years old (Dante's *mezzo del cammin*). It vividly expresses his shock at the suddenness of the loss of this central guide in his life. He is standing, on a dreary late autumn afternoon, outside the school chapel: "Coldly, sadly descends/The autumn evening. The field/strewn with its dank yellow drifts/Of wither'd leaves…" Inside is his father's tomb:

> There thou dost lie, in the gloom
> Of the autumn evening. But *ah!*
> That word, gloom, to my mind
> Brings thee back, in the light
> Of that radiant vigour, again;
> In the gloom of November we pass'd
> Days not dark by thy side;
> Seasons impair'd not the ray
> Of thy buoyant cheerfulness clear.
> Such thou wast! and I stand
> In the autumn evening, and think
> Of bygone autumns with thee.
>
> Fifteen years have gone round
> Since thou chosest to tread,
> In the summer-morning, the road
> Of death, at a call unforeseen,
> Sudden. For fifteen years,
> We who till then in thy shade
> Rested as under the boughs
> Of a mighty oak, have endured
> Sunshine and rain as we might,
> Bare, unshaded, alone,
> Lacking the shelter of thee.

When, twelve years earlier, Arnold was elected to a Fellowship at Oriel, it was a matter of some significance and pleasure to him that the date of his election (March 28th) coincided precisely with the thirtieth anniversary of his father's election to a fellowship at the same college. Similarly, when, in the same year he composed 'Rugby Chapel', he was elected to the Oxford Professorship of Poetry (a largely honorary appointment lasting ten years), he reflected, in a letter to his mother, how his father "would have rejoiced in his son's thus obtaining a share in the permanence and grandeur of that *august* place which he loved so much...This doubles the worth of the distinction in my eyes..." [2]

Arnold's career as a poet began early. One of his relatively few triumphs at Rugby was winning the Sixth Form Poetry Prize for 'Alaric at Rome'. A few years later at Oxford he won the prestigious Newdigate Prize for 'Cromwell' (subsequent winners were to include Oscar Wilde, Laurence Binyon, Julian Huxley and Andrew Motion). Not all of his poetic output can be described as readily accessible to a modern audience, but in poems such as 'Dover Beach', 'A Wish', and 'Growing Old', the expression of feeling is direct and raises vital questions as much for us as for his contemporary readers. In 'Empedocles on Etna', Arnold takes the legend of the Greek philosopher Empedocles throwing himself into the live crater of Mount Etna (to prove, according to one version of the legend, that he was immortal), and imagines his final hours. Arnold's Empedocles contemplates the gap between human aspirations and the indifference of the universe (which Camus was later to label the Absurd), the refusal of man to tolerate that gap and the invention of gods to fill the void. Here, the final plunge into the crater is presented, not as a nihilistic life-repudiating denial of ultimate meaning (as Camus pointed out, if life is absurd, suicide is no less so), but an act of salvation and purification, since in its consumption by fire, the body returns to the basic elements of which everything is made:

> To the elements it came from
> Everything will return -
> Our bodies to earth,
> Our blood to water,
> Heat to fire,
> Breath to air.
> They were well born, they will be well entombed—

There is, however, a problem:

> But mind, but thought—
> If these have been the master part of us -

---

[2] Letter to Mary Penrose Arnold, May 10, 1857. Lang (1996), p. 357.

> Where will *they* find their parent element?
> What will receive *them*, who will call *them* home?

A disturbing thought now occurs to Empedocles: perhaps our souls will not be freed from the enslavement of matter, but will be forced to undergo "the sad probation" over and over again, "And each succeeding age in which we are born/Will have more peril for us than the last". But then the cloud lifts, and he sees that he will at last be free:

> —Ah, boil up, ye vapours!
> Leap and roar, thou sea of fire!
> My soul glows to meet you.
> Ere it flag, ere the mists
> Of despondency and gloom
> Rush over it again,
> Receive me, save me!

The perennial problem of bodily death and its consequences for the life of the soul is grappled with in 'Rugby Chapel', this time with a much more personal edge:

> O strong soul, by what shore
> Tarriest thou now? For that force,
> Surely, has not been in vain!
> Somewhere, surely afar,
> In the sounding labour-house vast
> Of being, is practised that strength,
> Zealous, beneficent, firm!

But Arnold knew the bleak answer to that riddle.

In the *Manchester Guardian* obituary of his elder brother, Tom Arnold suggested that Matthew had lost his Christian faith by 1845, the year of his election at Oriel. But although Arnold is associated with those Victorian agnostics, like Clough and Leslie Stephen, who suffered a traumatic loss of faith, he arrived at an understanding of religion and the Bible that enabled him to continue to profess himself a Christian to the end of his life. Having virtually abandoned poetry as his preferred mode of expression, he published in the 1870s a series of writings offering a radical reinterpretation of religion which, nonetheless, strove to connect it with early Christianity and the religion of the Hebrew Bible. The original preface to *Literature and Dogma* (1873) opens with these stirring words:

> An inevitable revolution, of which we all recognise the beginning and signs, but which has already spread, perhaps, farther than most of us think, is befalling the religion in which we have been brought up….In no country will it be more felt than in England. This cannot be otherwise. It cannot be but that that the revolution should come, and that it should be here felt passionately, profoundly, painfully.[3]

What is this revolution, and why should it be particularly be felt in England? The crisis concerns the moral basis of the Bible, which in England (though of course not solely there) was asserted by ministers of religion to derive from direct inspiration by a "Great Personal First Cause." But now "many of the most successful, energetic and ingenious of the artisan class"[4] were now increasingly questioning the reason and authority for the things they had been taught to believe, in political and religious matters. And finding the supposed authority of the Bible doubtful, they were inclined to reject it altogether, and to regard it as an "exploded superstition." It was therefore a matter of urgency to show that the traditional axiomatic basis of the Bible must go, and to replace it with a quite different understanding of its origins, meaning and purpose in order for its potential for moral influence to be preserved.

The key themes of *Literature and Dogma* are these. First, the true object of religion is *conduct*—how to live rightly—rather than doctrine or dogma, concerning matters of cosmogony, for example. Arnold quotes a number of senior churchmen of the time as insisting on the importance of dogma as the backbone of religion, without which it would, they argued, be a nerveless thing. But Arnold points out that dogma involves reference to such abstruse notions as substance, causation, identity and design, the nature of which is a matter of debate, to which no fixed conclusion could be expected. And this would make our salvation dependent on something only few individuals could be supposed to possess, namely an ability to grasp and reason about such matters. Second, and relatedly, we should take a literary over a scientific

---

[3] Arnold (1873), p. 7.
[4] *Ibid.*, p. 9.

approach to Scripture. To talk scientifically is to use terms which can be given precise meanings, in order to make definite assertions about the world. To talk in a literary fashion is to use terms with fluid meanings, not primarily to make assertions, but to bring about a certain practical effect. Applying these two principles, Arnold defines religion as *morality touched with emotion*.[5] The scientific definition of God as "an infinite and eternal substance, and at the same time a person, the great first cause, the moral and intelligent governor of the universe"[6] is rejected in favour of a "power that makes for conduct or righteousness."[7]

It is perhaps unfair to complain that these definitions of religion and God lack precision, for he has just explained that the insistence on precision is a mark of the scientific. But we do need a bit more help in understanding them. By way of explanation of the difference between what we might call 'mere' morality and religion, he gives some examples. Here is one: "'Hold off from sensuality,' says Cicero; 'for, if you have given yourself up to it, you will find yourself unable to think of anything else.' That is morality. 'Blessed are the pure in heart,' says Jesus Christ; 'for they shall see God.' That is religion."[8] This is not terribly helpful, since the example makes explicit mention of God, and although we would not hesitate to describe that notion as 'religious', it does not make clear why, in Arnold's terms, it counts as religious. The difference is better explained as the difference between the cool expression of a moral code, and the expression of an ideal by means which also express a feeling. One does not, in religious utterance and activity, simply perceive a moral ideal, one experiences it as a passion.

When Arnold says that God as something "*not ourselves which makes for righteousness*",[9] it sounds as if he is advancing a metaphysical hypothesis: the postulation of some object independent of human thought which causes us to perceive the good and act on that perception. But this cannot be his intention, for that would again be to adopt a scientific approach. Rather, this is a characterisation of our own experience: we feel this power for goodness as if it were outside us, something greater than us, and so God is born as a

---

[5] *Ibid.*, p. 47.
[6] *Ibid.*, p. 38.
[7] *Ibid.*, 77.
[8] *Ibid.*, pp. 48-9.
[9] *Ibid.*, p. 82.

mythical projection. The presentation of moral feelings as directed towards a supreme being is, he says:

> a kind of fairy-tale, which a man tells himself, which no one, we grant, can prove impossible to turn out true, but which no one also can prove certain to turn out true. It is exactly what is expressed by the German word 'Aberglaube'—*extra belief*, belief beyond what is certain and verifiable.[10]

In sum, the language of God is a fictional language; we do not know how much of it is true, but with it we express our passionate acceptance of what we should do, and by it we bring ourselves to do what we should. That same message, proclaimed a century later by John Robinson in *Honest to God* (1963) and Don Cupitt in *Taking Leave of God* (1980) and *The Sea of Faith* (1984), evoked a storm of protest. The only significant difference between these and Arnold, is that the later writers were ordained ministers of the Anglican church, and Arnold was not. It seems that Arnold's revolution is taking much longer than he imagined.

Arnold's conception of religion was a wide one, as was his conception of culture, expressed in an earlier essay, *Culture and Anarchy* (1867-9). Culture, he explains, is often confused with little more than "a smattering of Greek and Latin", and something which operates primarily as "an engine of social and class distinction, separating its holder, like a badge or title, from other people who have not got it".[11] In contrast to these narrow conceptions, he offers this definition:

> a pursuit of our total perfection by means of getting to know, on all the matters which most concern us, the best which has been thought and said in the world; and through this knowledge, turning a stream of fresh and free thought upon our stock notions and habits, which we now follow staunchly but mechanically....[12]

More briefly, culture is simply the study of perfection, and its effect the perfection of humanity.

---

[10] *Ibid.*, p. 112.
[11] Arnold (1867-9), p. 43.
[12] *Ibid.*, p. 6.

Culture and Anarchy introduces a distinction between two modes of thought, which Arnold, whether fairly or unfairly, associates with two ancient civilisations: "The governing idea of Hellenism is *spontaneity of consciousness*; that of Hebraism, *strictness of conscience*."[13] His daily life afforded him extensive experience of the latter, as his full-time occupation—severely restricting the time available for his literary activities—was that of Inspector of Schools. This was a role he had taken out of necessity, for he had in 1849 met, and fallen in love with, Frances Lucy ('Flu') Wightman, but when the question of marriage arose, her father made it clear that he would not approve the match until Arnold had found himself a steady, and well-paid, position. What followed were thirty-six years of happy marriage, and thirty-five of sometimes irksome toil, travelling up and down the country's railways visiting Nonconformist schools.

In contrast to the misconception of culture he was opposing, Arnold's conception is inclusivist rather than elitist. It seeks not to divide but to unify. And when he talks of the best that has been thought and said in the world, he suggests a truly global range of influences. Rather than reinforcing the status quo, those influences challenge it, by bringing fresh ideas and practices to our conventional outlook. Finally, the object of culture is the perfection of the individual human being, and this perfection, he explains, is to be seen as "an *internal* condition of the mind and spirit"[14] rather than social progress, although the effect of that internal condition is social progress of the best kind.

This famous characterisation of culture makes interesting comparison with the principles of Olympism, as articulated by the International Olympic Academy, founded just six years after Arnold's death. These principles are not simply a code of practice for the running of a four-yearly event; they constitute a moral ideal which is intended to inform all sporting activity and sport education. "Olympism", explains the first principle, "seeks to create a way of life based on the joy of effort, the educational value of good example, social responsibility and respect for universal fundamental ethical principles."[15] Among those ethical principles concern the rights of the individual, and sport among those human rights. "Every individual must

---

[13] *Ibid.*, p. 132.
[14] *Ibid.*, p. 49.
[15] International Olympic Committee (2011).

have the possibility of practicing sport, without discrimination of any kind."[16] Like Arnold's view of culture, then, Olympism is inclusivist, not elitist. The goal of sport, like the goal of culture, is the perfection of the individual human being, though sport adds the perfection of the human body to that of the mind. That is aiming at an internal condition. But the ultimate aim of Olympism, like the ultimate effect of culture, is an external one: the improvement of human nature in general and a peaceful society.

To be a true Olympian is not, primarily, to excel in one's chosen activity, but to subscribe wholeheartedly to the principles of Olympism. And those principles are quite general ones, not applicable only to sporting activity. Matthew Arnold, then, is a true cultural Olympian, not because of the undoubted importance of his contribution to culture, but because his conception of culture is itself Olympian.

Tom Arnold remarked that his brother felt himself to be doomed, having inherited the weakness of heart that had killed his father. The end, when it came, was swift: on April 15th, 1888, Arnold collapsed suddenly on his way to meet his daughter, who had just arrived in Liverpool after an Atlantic crossing. He died within minutes. To that extent, he was granted what he had expressed in *A Wish*, where he imagines one on his death-bed asking to be spared the stream of mourners at the bedside, the "doctor full of phrase and fame", and "His brother doctor of the soul". But, in a passage that conveys Arnold's ultimately joyful yet realistic view of life, the poem ends with the request to be carried to the window, where the dying man can see:

> Bathed in the sacred dew of morn
> The wide aerial landscape spread—
> The world which was ere I was born,
> The world which lasts when I am dead.
>
> Which never was the friend of *one*,
> Nor promised love it could not give,
> But lit for all its generous sun,
> And lived itself, and made us live.

---

[16] *Ibid.*

Bibliography

Allott, Kenneth (1965) ed., *The Poems of Matthew Arnold*. London: Longman.

Arnold, Matthew (1867-9) *Culture and Anarchy*. Ed. J. Dover Wilson. Cambridge: Cambridge University Press, 1932.

Arnold, Matthew (1873) *Literature and Dogma*. London: Thomas Nelson and Sons 1915.

Arnold, Thomas, the younger (1888) 'Matthew Arnold', *Manchester Guardian*, May 18th, 1888

Cupitt, Don (1984). *The Sea of Faith: Christianity in Change*. London: BBC Publications.

Hamilton, Ian (1998) *A Gift Imprisoned: the Poetic Life of Matthew Arnold*. London: Bloomsbury.

International Olympic Committee (2011). *The Olympic Charter*. Lausanne: IOC.

Lang, Cecil Y. (1996) *The Letters of Matthew Arnold, Volume I: 1829-59*. Charlottesville: University Press of Virginia.

Murray, Nicholas (1996) *A Life of Matthew Arnold*. London: Hodder and Stoughton.

Lewis Carroll and Victorian Controversy

A N Wilson

Even when we take into account the fact that Salman Rushdie became a household name after writing *The Satanic Verses*, and even if Rupert Brooke's "The Soldier" was once an anthology-piece as well-known as Kipling's "If", it remains true that Lewis Carroll is without any rival the most famous author to have attended Rugby School. In every corner of the globe where Matthew Arnold and Arthur Hugh Clough are only known to students of literature, there are millions of people who have heard of *Alice's Adventures in Wonderland*. If R.H. Tawney, or R.G. Collingwood or T.H. Green are luminaries of British intellectual history, their legacy, though enduring, is for the most part hidden. As Lewis Carroll, however, Charles Lutwidge Dodgson was in a different category. Yet of course, this both is and is not the case. For Dodgson was an academic all his life. He lived his adult life in a city, Oxford, where the questions of faith and science, reason and revelation, logic and the Condition of England were hotly contested along party lines. These were matters which broke friendships, and tore lives in two. The controversies, as they tore Oxford, and the nation, in two, would lead to Newman's life of exile (on the one hand); to Jowett's reform of the University system on the other. Honest Doubt would project Morley or Froude into the life of Men of Letters, and allow cynical old Mark Pattison to a life of acidic seclusion in Turl Street.

Throughout the turbulent years of nineteenth century intellectual conflict, the Reverend Charles Dodgson, who was made deacon by that selfsame Samuel Wilberforce, Bishop of Oxford ("Soapy Sam") who had disputed with Huxley about the implications of Darwinism, continued to give his mathematical lectures, and to write his books of logic and mathematics – *The Fifth Book of Euclid treated Algebraically* by "A College Tutor" (1858); or *A Syllabus of Plane Algebraical Geometry* (1860), down to *The Game of Logic* in 1887.

In June 1862, as all the world knows, Dodgson, in the company of his most celebrated "child friend", Alice Liddell, went for a picnic and first told the stories which became *Alice's Adventures Underground*. When he yielded to their pleading, and wrote the stories down, his life was changed.

The first of his academic textbooks was written anonymously – by "A College Tutor", and the *Alice* books were written under a pseudonym. Dodgson, a retiring, stammering figure, had no wish for celebrity; and we can infer from the choice of a pseudonym that it pleased him to keep his two identities in separate compartments. One man, the much-liked college-tutor, was what was called even in my day at Oxford a "Good College Man". As Curator of the Common Room at Christ Church, it was his care to make sure that the wine cellar was to the liking of the other dons; that the servants were filling up the coal scuttles and the ink wells, supplying them with writing paper, and excluding draughts. In that Common Room, Dodgson must have heard so many discussions, about the progress of Christ Church's greatest Prime Minister, William Ewart Gladstone, about the condition of the Church, about Science and Religion. Was it not in this very Common Room that the High Churchmen, inspired by their leader Dr Pusey, decided that the presence in the college of a stuffed Dodo might be injurious to the faith of wavering undergraduates? The taxidermal rarity was therefore destroyed, surviving only as a picture in the University's Natural History Museum in Park's Road.

Dodgson saw many a Caucus Race and Lobster Quadrille enacted in Tom Quad, and Peckwater, not to mention in the cloisters of the Cathedral itself, which serves as the College chapel. Are we to suppose that he spent the second half of the nineteenth century absorbed in algebraic puzzles, exercises in photography and child-friendships, while the great debates of the age floated unabsorbed above his head?

It was more or less exactly a century after John Keble's Assize Sermon of 1833, which is generally taken to be the opening salvo of the Oxford Movement, that Sir Shane Leslie published his provoking essay on "Lewis Carroll and the Oxford Movement" in the *London Mercury*. Of course, the paper is a spoof - "submitted to the Historical Theological School at Göttingen University", but like comparable learned jokes – one thinks of W.E. Gladstone's thesis that Dante had visited Oxford – it was based upon a close reading of the text, and the grasping of some kind of half-truth about the nature of the material.

"Lewis Carroll and the Oxford Movement" claims to have uncovered the "key" of the *Alice* books, which were published in 1865 and 1871 respectively. Leslie's contention was that the Reverend Charles Dodgson , a don at Christ Church and colleague of the venerable Dr Pusey, was writing an allegory of that religious movement which, from the 1830s onwards, had so rocked, not merely Oxford, but the Church of England, and which had known such dramas as the conversion of John Henry Newman and Henry Manning to Roman Catholicism, the development of the ritualistic or Puseyite strain of worship into the National Church, and, in the case of many early enthusiasts for Newman's charm and rhetoric – figures such as James Anthony Froude or Matthew Arnold – a reaction or lapse into scepticism.

Alice, according to Leslie's paper, "may be regarded as the simple Freshman or Everyman who wanders like a sweet and innocent Undergraduate into the Wonderland of a Victorian Oxford, where everyone was religious in some way or another". The White Rabbit is the type of average English clergyman, and the exotics whom Alice is to encounter represent differing strands of the Tractarian (named after the *Tracts for the Times* which excited national frenzy) or High Church controversy. So, we find that the Cheshire Cat is Cardinal Wiseman – "It looked good-natured, Alice thought, still it had very long claws and a great many teeth so she felt it ought to be treated with respect". The March Hare and the Hatter are, respectively, the Low Church and the High Church parties. The top hat was indeed a badge of High Church allegiance until the mid-twentieth century, and the Hatter's obsession with time may be taken as a spoof on High Church revivals of ancient ecclesiastical calendars. The Mock Turtle is a wistful High Church Victorian looking back to the time when there was "real" as opposed to merely aspirant Catholicism in its land – "Once I was a real Turtle....The Master was an Old Turtle. We used to call him Tortoise because he taught us" – a clear reference, Leslie professed to suppose – to the "Pope and the *ecclesia docens*". When he came to analyse *Through the Looking Glass*, Leslie was able actually to match characters in the story to figures of contemporary controversy – The White Queen to Newman, the Red Queen to Manning, the White King to Benjamin Jowett, great Master of Balliol, and the White Knight to Thomas Huxley, and so on.

Such an amusing exercise as Leslie's will probably not bring help us to appreciate the *Alice* stories any more intelligently than would an attempt to persuade us that there is a political or historical allegory at work – for example, that Dodgson intended allusion to the so-called Bedchamber Crisis of 1839, when Queen Victoria quarrelled with Peel about the composition of her intimate court. And yet, as the mainstream Lewis Carroll scholars and biographers have shown us, that there is a direct link between the evolution of the stories, and Dodgson's own life is beyond question. Dodgson, who came into residence at Christ Church in 1851, who was nominated the next year – by Dr Pusey – to a Studentship (ie Fellowship), who took his First in Mathematics two years later, was a maths and logic don all his adult life. It hardly needs to be said that there really was an Alice – Alice Liddell, daughter of the Dean of Christ Church, and that it was on that picnic, taken with the Liddells on June 17th, 1862, when Alice was seven, that Dodgson first told the story of *Alice's Adventures Underground*. Many of the figures within, such as Dinah the Cat, were real, or thinly disguised versions of real characters. The Dodo was Dodgson's own nickname, the Duck was obviously his friend Duckworth (the Reverend Robinson Duckworth, Fellow of Trinity)who accompanied them on the original picnic, and it seems fair to accept the suggestion made by Roger Lancelyn Green in his learned edition of the stories[1] that, for example, the children's Governess Miss Prickett suggested both the Mouse in *Wonderland* and the Red Queen in *Through the Looking-Glass*; and that the Drawling Master who was "an old conger eel, that used to come once a week" is intended as a (perhaps slightly bitchy) reference to John Ruskin: "he taught us Drawling, Stretching and Fainting in Coils", an almost Joycean sentence which surely doubles mere verbal doodling with a recollection of the passionate intensity and neurosis of that genius Ruskin.

Leslie Stephen's joke, therefore, both teaches us how NOT to read Lewis Carroll – as pure allegory – but alerts us to the life of things which both feeds the stories and which remains having a life of its own beneath the surface. A story by an English clergyman about someone who comes across a bottle with a paper label reading DRINK ME; and who furthermore discovered a box with a "very small cake on which the words EAT ME were beautifully marked in currants" can scarcely avoid arousing a memory, however tenuous, of the central command of the Christian Eucharist. Likewise, many of the sharp exchanges between Alice and the creatures whom she encounters, while not being anything so crude as satires or allegories on contemporary academic discourse, surely reflect his experience of living among them. Who could read the *Tracts for the Times*, and note the intensity with which such matters as Baptismal Regeneration, or the retranslation of the Psalms, could be discussed, could fail to catch an echo of such habits of mind in the White Queen. "Why, sometimes I've believed as many as six impossible things before breakfast". It was at early chapel, or the "early service" before breakfast that the Eucharist was celebrated. The necessity of fasting communions, and of obeying the injunction to "Eat Me" before the consumption of breakfast, which was a key feature of High Church piety.

---

[1] Lewis Carroll: *Alice's Adventures in Wonderland and Through the Looking Glass*, Edited with an Introduction by Roger Lancelyn Green, Oxford University Press, 1971.

You do not have to believe Sir Shane Leslie's spoof to suppose that the bizarre atmosphere of High Church Oxford is the soil in which it grew. And central to both the Alice stories, almost their theme of themes, is the bizarre way in which a young mind receives information, processes statements and propositions, tests the limits of language. To this extent, it is immediately recognizeable as a profoundly philosophical work – not in the sense of a book which wishes to propose a particular view of life, but as one which makes a comedy out of "language truth and logic" – to use a phrase popularized by a later alumnus of Christ Church. –

"When *I* use a word", Humpty Dumpty said, in rather a scornful tone, "it means just what I choose it to mean – neither more nor less". "The question is", said Alice, "whether you *can* make words mean so many different things". One of the intellectually thrilling features of Carroll's comedy is the way in which it is both a teasing recollection of a real little girl in a Victorian school-room, and atthe same time an exploration of the foundations of knowledge. Metaphysical questions which absorbed Plato in the *Meno*- how does a brain learn? Is learning simply recollection? – appear to leap forward and anticipate a much later generation of philosophical discourse – that of Wittgenstein or Gilbert Ryle.

Charles Dodgson's father, whose career at Oxford antedated the Tractarian revival, was nonetheless wholly in sympathy with it. His churchmanship was High and Dry, but he believed it was the priest's job, "to spend all and be spent in the single work of winning souls to Christ". It is surely plausible to suppose that it was the younger Dodgson's inability quite to aspire to such solemnity which prevented him from proceeding to ordination to the priesthood, remaining in Deacon's orders. (The diffidence was intensified by Charles Dodgson's paralysing stammer; or should we say that the stammer was what enabled and justified the diffidence?) . Charles Lutwidge Dodgson clearly loved his father, and enjoyed on what might be called a Trollopian level, the grander by-ways of the National Church. His father's early friendship with Longley, to whom he owed his Canonry at Ripon, continued when Longley became Archbishop of Canterbury. Longley indeed was Carroll's most-photographed male sitter.[2]

---

[2] J.R.Garrard "Charles Thomas Longley", Oxford Dictionary of National Biuography, Volume 34, (2004), p.401

When Longley died on October 27th, 1868, he was succeeded as the Primate of All England by Lewis Carroll's old Rugby Headmaster, Archibald Campbell Tait. As a tutor at Balliol in the early 1840s, Tait had been in the vanguard of those dons who attacked Newman, for his suggestion, in the notorious Tract XC that more or less full-blown Catholicism was compatible with membership of the Church of England. A robust liberal in the Arnoldian mould Tait was a Rugbeian "natural". Yet although a (Thomas) Arnoldian, and the tutor of Benjamin Jowett, Tait was to harden, as a bishop and Archbishop into something rather different. While relatively at ease with the developments in science and textual critcisim of the Bible which rocked the faith of so many of his contemporaries, Tait, who had been a popular Balliol tutor, became an intolerant Prince of the Church. He publicly and in some ways offensively disowned his two old pupils Jowett- later Master of Balliol – and Frederick Temple – later to succeed him as Headmaster of Rugby; and he openly advocated the criminal prosecution of ritualists (Dr Pusey's friends) after the Public Worship Regulation Act came into force in 1874. Charles Lutwidge Dodgson thought the ritualists were absurd, but what would Lewis Carroll have made of a Judge in full-bottomed wig, being addressed by barristers in robes and wigs, prosecuting and sending to prison a clergyman who chose to wear other robes – no doubt equally arcane to the uninitiated eye – while conducting his religious duties?

Charles Dodgson had not been a happy schoolboy as a pupil of Tait's at Rugby, though such was his gentleness and respect for his father that he did not reveal this fact until long after he had left. He described school to his younger brothers as "learning lessons in fear of the birch"[3]. A pre-Arnoldian pupil at Rugby described the teaching methods as books being learnt by heart and recited, "without so far as I can recall, a word of explanation or illustration. The lists of the Kings of England, of the metals, and of the planets were repeated one after the other without interest and without discrimination". Although Arnold was to introduce into the Rugby curriculum mathematics and modern languages, the meaningless learning by rote of an earlier period no doubt survived into Dodgson's schooldays. One of the especially brilliant things about the *Alice* books is the way in which they convey a young mind absorbing words, poems, snatches of historical and other knowledge, without the smallest comprehension and, by only the smallest variants and variations, transforming them into pure nonsense.

---

[3] Donald Thomas, *Lewis Carroll A Portrait with Background*, 1996, p. 52

It was in mathematics that the young Dodgson immediately flourished. The Reverend Robert Bickersteth Mayor, who was principal master in the subject when Dodgson was at the school, wrote to Dodgson pere in 1848, "I have not had a more promising boy at his age since I came to Rugby".

Charles won prizes in almost every subject, including for mathematics, before he reached the sixth form. He was ill in his last year at the school, suffering from whooping cough and mumps, and it was probably this which caused his father to remove him from the school slightly early, just before his seventeenth birthday.

There is the stutter. Hellish at the best of times, to be afflicted with a stammer , or any form of speech-oddity at school is an everlasting torment which other children pick upon, imitate, or, even if they are perfectly good-humoured, make worse by <u>noticing.</u> One of the tricks which a stutterer develops very necessarily is the art of word-substitution, so that if the desired word is not forthcoming, another can plausibly be pronounced, rather than hesitated over. Frances Huxley in *The Raven and the Writing Desk* (1976) brilliantly explored the phenomenon of substitution among stutterers. If the intelligent stutterer sees a "difficult" word approaching in the sentence which he or she is uttering, they will supply another word – and it is possible to read a poem like "The Hunting of the Snark" as just such an exercise in substitution. But if one word substitutes for another – are we not in the world of Humpty Dumpty once again? How do we make signifiers signify?

Dodgson's father, the old High Churchman of Ripon, persuaded Dr Pusey at Christ Church to make him what was called an undergraduate student, that is to make him a sort of apprentice fellow of the college before he had so much as arrived there. Members of Christ Church, the *Aedes Christi*, call it "the House", and from the moment of his arrival there, Dodgson junior regarded it as a home, and found in it both the intellectual stimulus and a home – of sorts. As an Oxford College it had many noted peculiarities. Not merely was its chapel a Cathedral, a high proportion of its Students (ie fellows) were Canons of that Cathedral, and , being Canon-Professors, they were permitted to marry, unlike the junior dons who were celibates. "The House", therefore, had families,; it was not just a collection of mad bachelors. And presiding over them all was the Dean, with his daughters, the "child friends".

Though it would be crass to see the *Alice* stories as a satire or even as a skit upon Christianity, we note a certain impenetrable attitude which was exasperating to his clerical colleagues. In 1867, Dodgson had a notable holiday in St Petersburgh with Henry Parry Liddon, a high church zealot, later Dean of St Paul's, who would grow to become Dr Pusey's representative on earth. It was on this holiday that Dodgson told Liddon that he objected to the use of the term "Catholic" to apply to members of the Church of England because "it connected us with Rome". Liddon in turn was scandalized by Dodgson's inability to stir himself before half past nine of a morning.[4] Dean Liddell, Alice's father, noted with disapproval that Dodgson never appeared at the early morning services in the college chapel – that is, Christ Church Cathedral. These [5] absences and these late mornings are suggestive, if not of open unbelief, then of creeping indifferentism. Or not even indifferentism, but a certain playfulness. Whether he believed anything before breakfast, he kept it to himself.

He was evidently not a sceptic in the sense that Huxley was. He was not, like Froude, disillusioned by the Oxford Movement since, while owing his position at Christ Church to Dr Pusey, he never displayed the slightest interest in Puseyism, nor in Evangelicalism, nor in the contemporary battles which so interested his holiday-companion Liddon, or in the controversies which so engaged his fellow-children's writer Charles Kingsley. Rather, the rhetoric of "Nonsense" allows him to adopt the selfsame attitude to the primary Christian texts and to the core doctrines of early Christianity as expressed in the Nicene Creed as he did to Euclid. "Is Euclid's Axiom True? The answer I propose to give to this alarming proposition is that, though true in the sense *he meant it*, it is *not* true in the sense in which *we take it*". [from Dodgson's *Curiosa Mathematica* Part II: *A New Theory of Parallels*,1888].

Dodgson was too conservative a man – small c conservative – to have patience with out and out scepticism, and too humorous a man to have sympathy with the hard-line bigots whose controversies formed so loud a background music to college life in his day. But this is not to say that the stories he told to Alice Liddell bore no relationship to those controversies. Academics and churchmen love controversy, but while the latter might have cultivated the controversial habit ever since Augustine argued with the

---

[4] Donald Thomas, p. 203
[5] Donald Thomas, p. 171

Donatists, or Athanasius argued for the Trinity, Carroll the teller of tales and good friend of childish minds surely is at one with Dodgson the tutor in Logic, when he saw that true academic discourse must always be open ended. We might not know why a Raven is like a Writing Desk. But we know why a philosophy tutorial should not be like a controversy; and why an essay in logic should not be like a *Tract for the Times*. An open mind, much as it would horrify Dr Pusey to hear us say it, is a mind ever open to change.

"Don't let us quarrel", the White Queen said in an anxious tone. "What is the cause of lightning?"

"The cause of lightning", Alice said very decidedly, for she felt certain about this, "is the thunder – no, no!" she hastily corrected herself, "I meant the other way".

"It's too late to correct it", said the Red Queen: "when you've once said a thing, that fixes it, and you must take the consequences".

T.H. Green: political and philosophical radical

Andrew Vincent

It is sometimes difficult to fully appreciate the general ethos of the Victorian era. We can still find their enthusiasms puzzling. The writing style (and interests) of someone like Thomas Carlyle or John Ruskin can now seem unduly florid or bombastic; although during their lives they were widely admired. As one late 20th century commentator has remarked, such ideas (as Green's) were often "embedded in a set of assumptions which no longer demand our allegiance, and addressed to a range of problems which no longer commands our attention."[1]

Green's reputation, over the last half century, has been somewhat eclipsed by contemporaneous Victorian philosophical luminaries, such as J.S. Mill or Henry Sidgwick. Yet we should not think that this reflects anything fundamental about the quality of the work. Assessments, over the last fifty years, say little about philosophical capability and more about the very different timbre of intellectual traditions. T.S. Eliot, who started his own doctoral study on one of Green's philosophical contemporaries, F.H. Bradley, remarking on the decline of the Idealist school in the late 1920s, noted that although such philosophy "is today a little out of fashion, we must remark that what has superseded it, what is now in favour is, for the most part, crude and raw and provincial (though infinitely more technical and scientific) and must perish in its turn."[2] It is clear though that the Idealist philosophy that Green espoused was rejected by mainstream academic traditions from the late 1920s and 1930s, and it has only recently begun to be seriously studied again.

There are noteworthy biographical overlaps between T.H. Green and another *Olympian* in this present volume. Both Sidgwick and Green were sons of Church of England clergy in Yorkshire. Sidgwick's father died when he was three, in Green's case his mother died when he was one year old, in 1837. Green was educated by his father, the Rev. Valentine Green, Rector of Birkin in Yorkshire, and was sent to Rugby school when he was fourteen in 1850; Sidgwick went in 1852. Rugby School had fairly recently been reformed by Dr. Thomas Arnold. Both young men became fairly accomplished linguists, German being one language they cultivated in common. They indeed became friends at Rugby and later travelled in Germany together, although their reactions to German philosophy and culture were quite different. Sidgwick went to Cambridge University and Green to Balliol in Oxford, both in 1855. They performed well in their respective degrees and Sidgwick was elected a fellow in 1859 and Green appointed lecturer in ancient and modern history in 1860, and in November of that year was elected a fellow at Balliol. Both Sidgwick and Green

---

[1] Stefan Collini, *Liberals and Sociology: L.T. Hobhouse and Political Argument in England 1880-1915* (Cambridge: Cambridge University Press, 1979), p.253.
[2] T.S. Eliot, 'Francis Herbert Bradley' in *Eliot, For Lancelot Andrews: Essays on Style and Order* (London: Faber and Faber, 1928/1970), p.60.

struggled with the idea of signing the 39 Articles of the Church of England - a prerequisite for becoming a university fellow, until the repeal of the requirement in 1871. Both also wrestled – virtually throughout their lives - with orthodox Christianity, particularly with mainstream Christian beliefs. Whereas Green formulated a fairly rounded response on this issue, within his own Idealist-inspired liberal theology, Sidgwick floundered uncomfortably in psychic research. Both developed quite opposed philosophical positions: Sidgwick became the doyen of sophisticated analytically-orientated utilitarianism and Green the key founder of the philosophical school of British Idealism. Their early friendship did become strained in later years. Oddly, whereas Green did not really engage directly with Sidgwick's philosophy - although he did criticize utilitarianism - Sidgwick did preoccupy himself quite directly with Green's philosophy. He regarded Green as the ablest exponent of Idealism in Britain – a philosophy he felt deep antipathy for. Sidgwick's last essay in *Mind* in 1901, which was published the year after his death, was yet another attempt to refute Green's idealism (Green had in fact died some twenty years earlier in 1882).[3]

i

At Rugby Green was never a model pupil. As his biographer R.L. Nettleship remarked, between his headmaster Dr. Goulbourn and himself, "there was little sympathy or mutual appreciation."[4] Green was neither competitive nor ambitious; if anything he was constitutionally indolent. Most academic subjects he studied at Rugby did not excite him and competitive sports struck him as futile. The only occasion he really shone was when the subject matter fully engaged his intellect. Thus, he acquired a prize for Latin prose at Rugby with a passage drawn from Milton's *Areopagitica*.

What really marked Green out during this period was a mental independence, which stayed with him throughout his life. He retained a firm belief in freedom of thought, which Nettleship remarks, "gave him a peculiar impressiveness to a small number."[5] He disliked unreasoned authority. His friends at Rugby thus noted in him a "certain solid wilfulness, a certain grave

---

[3] Henry Sidgwick, 'The Philosophy of T.H. Green' *Mind*, vol 10, N.S. (1901).
[4] R.L. Nettleship, *Memoir* in Nettleship (ed.) *Works of Thomas Hill Green Vol III* (London: Longmans, Green and Co, 1888), p.xiv.
[5] Nettleship, *Memoir*, p.xv.

rebelliousness", as well as a "strong sympathy with the weak and friendless."[6] He liked to be alone with his own ruminations and would go for long walks on his own on Sundays. He commented that "he could worship best in the green fields by himself."[7] He did though have one singular reputation at school. He was seen by many contemporaries as the "politician" of the school and was most effective in the school debating society. Indeed, he was often viewed - both in Rugby and Oxford - as a "dreadful radical". His preferred reading at school was the work of F.D Maurice, Thomas Carlyle and Charles Kingsley. His Carlyleian hero was Oliver Cromwell. In fact, he retained a passionate historical and philosophical interest in intellectual Puritanism, the English civil war and the Commonwealth, throughout his working life, as can be seen from his later *Four Lectures on the English Commonwealth*.[8] He was also inclined to distrust Catholicism and retained a distaste for High Churchmanship. As a University teacher he was consequently disapproving of his students - particularly in one notable case the later Jesuit poet Gerard Manley Hopkins - moving towards Catholicism.[9]

His view of Balliol and Oxford University was also initially negative. Green remarked that "The inside of the [Oxford] colleges are strangely incongruous with the outside. The finest colleges are the most corrupt, the functionaries from the heads to the servants being wholly given to quiet dishonesty, and the undergraduates to sensual idleness."[10] Green clearly felt deeply uneasy with the preoccupations of many of his fellow undergraduates. He was irritated with their sporting focus, drinking culture (he was largely teetotal), and their arrogant sense of superiority. He confessed on many occasions that he felt much more at ease with ordinary working people, farmers and tradesman than Oxford staff or students. Something that became more pronounced in later life was his intense view of social equality as a religious, moral and political ideal. His austere demeanour often made him appear unsocial and aloof to some fellow students, although Nettleship

---

[6] Nettleship, *Memoir*, p.xiv.
[7] Nettleship, *Memoir*, p.xvi.
[8] Green, 'Four Lectures on the English CommonWealth' in *Works*, Vol III, pp.277-364.
[9] See T.H. Green letter to Scott Holland in Paget, S. (ed) *Henry Scott Holland: Memoir and Letters* (London: John Murray, 1921), pp.31-2.
[10] Green quoted in Nettleship *Memoir*, p.xvi.

remarks, that for those who knew him well, he was consistently a "delightful companion", humorous, genial and very sympathetic.[11]

As in Rugby, Green found many of his subjects and tutors at University disappointing. However a solid difference was made with this personal tutor Benjamin Jowett (later Master of Balliol) and the Professor of Latin, John Conington. To both he acknowledged a lasting debt of gratitude. Jowett, at the time, was still subject to harsh criticism for his theological views and Green implicitly admired his courage and intellectual stance. It was Jowett, in all probability, who started Green reading German philosophy.

Many of the intellectual themes, which later became highly characteristic of Green's position, can be seen in his student years. He remained a radical liberal. He retained a strong concern for the poor and had little but "contempt... for those theories of national honour and greatness which are, it is true, only the expression of political vanity."[12] In a noteworthy passage, in one his early papers on "National Life" (1858), delivered to a discussion group – The Old Mortality Society - Green remarked starkly: "Let the flag of England be dragged through the dirt rather than sixpence be added to the taxes which weight on the poor."[13] Green expressed similar views in the Oxford Union debates, which made him an unpopular speaker for many of his more aristocratic and conservative-minded fellow students.

Green – as indicated - became a fellow of Balliol in 1860. In 1863 he refused, on Jowett's advice, an offer of the editorship of the *Times of India*. On Jowett's election as Master of Balliol in 1870 Green took over the subordinate management of Balliol College. In 1878 he was elected to the Whyte's professorship of moral philosophy in Oxford, he stayed in this post until his early death in 1882.

ii

Green's legacy can be identified in four domains. The first of these is philosophy. Green's major published works were a comprehensive introduction to an edition of *The Philosophical Works of David Hume* (1874-5) with T.H. Grose as joint editor; the *Prolegomena to Ethics* ed. A.C. Bradley

---

[11] Nettleship, *Memoir*, p.xix.
[12] Nettleship, *Memoir*, xxi.
[13] Green quoted in Nettleship, *Memoir*, pp. xx-xxi.

(1883); *The Witness of God, and Faith. Two Lay Sermons*, ed. Arnold Toynbee (1883), which contains the famous lay sermons delivered at Balliol; *The Works of Thomas Hill Green*, Vols I-III, ed. R.L. Nettleship (1885-8). *Lectures on the Principles of Political Obligation*, reprinted from Volume II of the *Works* (1895). Apart from the Hume introduction, all Green's major works were edited and published after his death by ex-students.

In Green's own day Oxford was still dominated by classics and in philosophy by Aristotelianism. The Oxford examination statute of 1850 contained no mention of Kant or Hegel, or J.S. Mill for that matter. It was not until 1875 that the first questions on Kant and Hegel appeared, due largely to Green's influence.

Green was primarily interested in the philosophies of Kant, Fichte and Hegel, although it is ironic that he was one of the first to advocate the serious academic study of David Hume in Britain. Green saw most of the defects of empiricism (including Hume's) and naturalism through Kantian eyes. The most important philosophical question was Kantian, namely, "how is knowledge possible?" For Green, the self-conscious agent is the precondition to knowledge. The problem, for Green, was Kant's doctrine of the manifold, independent of the agent. Kant wanted to retain the idea of a world independent of consciousness which cannot be known in itself. Following Hegel, Green argued that Kant had fallen into an unnecessary dualism. There was no need to postulate a world independent of the determinations of judgment. The Kantian "thing-in-itself" did not exist for Green. He took a similar line in his work on Aristotle. For Green, Aristotle's theory of knowledge and his account of matter would have been improved immeasurably if he had realised that knowledge of things implies judgment and in every judgment the self-conscious subject is implied.

It was the Kantian agent which also formed the starting point for Green's cryptic Hegelianism. The major theme that Green developed from Hegel was the idea that *Reason* (or as Green called it "the eternal consciousness") was the metaphysical unity implicit in the world. The aim of the philosopher was thus to articulate the *Reason* of the world. If Green read Aristotle through Kantian eyes, he often read Kant through Hegelian eyes. The self-conscious agent thus presupposed, via a transcendental argument, an eternal consciousness or unifying Spirit, equivalent to Hegel's notion of *Geist* (spirit). The "eternal consciousness" was the presupposition to the unity of knowledge of individual self-conscious agents.[14] However Green was not uncritical of Hegel. He repudiated the idea that Hegel had discovered some fundamental secret of the universe. Green, in fact, often turned the tables, to read Hegel with Kantian eyes, reaffirming the central epistemological and moral role of the self-conscious agent.

As an Idealist, Green was always a rigorous critic of empiricism and naturalism. His characteristic philosophical approach was to argue that knowledge of the world and nature does not explain the nature of knowledge. Knowledge of the world exists for the self-conscious agent. For Green, empiricism and naturalism committed the fallacy of trying to identify the real outside of thought. Knowledge always presupposed a knower. Green's philosophical status was, for a time, pivotal. Every important philosopher in Britain between 1880 and 1914 responded to his work. This influence was not confined to Britain. His writings were considered seriously in the USA, Italy and Japan. Since the 1990s there has indeed been a decisive resurgence of interest.[15] In addition, Green made a crucial contribution to the professionalization of philosophy as a discipline in Oxford, encouraging a much more rigorous research orientated approach to the discipline and

---

[14] A central ambiguity, at this point, was that if the eternal consciousness reproduced itself through individual agents, then was the separate human agent merely an imperfect form of the eternal consciousness? This particular point became a bone of contention between Absolute and Personal Philosophical Idealists in Britain up to the early 1920s.

[15] There has been a new edition of his collected works: *The Collected Works of T.H. Green* eds. R.L. Nettleship and Peter Nicholson (Bristol: Thoemmes, 1997). There have also been a number of individual scholarly studies: Andrew Vincent and Raymond Plant, *Philosophy Politics and Citizenship* (Oxford: Blackwell 1984); G. Thomas, *The Moral Philosophy of T.H. Green* (Oxford: Clarendon Press, 1987); Maria Dimova-Cookson, *T.H. Green's Moral and Political Philosophy: A Phenomenological Perspective* (Basingstoke: Palgrave Macmillan, 2001); Matt Carter, *T.H. Green and the Development of Ethical Socialism* (Exeter: Imprint Academic, 2003); David O Brink, *Perfectionism and the Common Good: Themes in the Philosophy of T.H. Green* (Clarendon Press: Oxford, 2003); Ben Wempe, *T.H. Green's Theory of Positive Freedom* (Exeter: Imprint Academic, 2004); Denys P. Leighton *The Greenian Moment: T.H. Green, Religion and Political Argument in Victorian Britain*, (Exeter: Imprint Academic, 2004); Maria Dimova-Cookson and W.J. Mander eds. *T.H. Green: Ethics, Metaphysics and Political Philosophy* (Oxford: Clarendon Press, 2006); Alberto de Sanctis, *The 'Puritan' Democracy of Thomas Hill Green* (Exeter: Imprint Academic, 2005); Colin Tyler, *Civil Society, Capitalism and the State* (Exeter: Imprint Academic, 2012).

widening its sphere of operation to (what would now be called) continental philosophy.

iii

The second dimension of Green's legacy lies in ethics. The most complete statement is to be found in the *Prolegomena to Ethics* (1883). Some scholars, particularly those influenced by post-1940s philosophy, see ethics as the most philosophically reputable aspect of his thought. The central ethical concept is character. For Green moral action is the expression of character, which is a quality of the self implied in action. Green's ethics is also focused on self-realisation. The self is identified with latent capacities of the person. Humans distinguish themselves from animals by their ability to think about desires. The conceived desire is a motive. The self posits an object which will satisfy the conceived desire. The capacity to choose an object is the will. In all action an individual is positing an object which will satisfy the conceived desires. The satisfaction is described as a "good." However, the "true good" is that object which provides complete satisfaction, which is the full realisation of the potentialities of the self. Such a realisation cannot be identified with pleasure. Pleasure or happiness may be a by-product of moral action, but cannot be the end of it. The self cannot be identified with discrete sensations, since the self is the presupposition to any sensations. This is a basic point underpinning his rejection of utilitarian ethics, although some twentieth century commentators have argued that Green is, despite appearances, more sympathetic to utilitarianism than is often supposed. Overall Green's ethics can be identified with a perfectionist tradition which combines a rigorous critical attack on naturalism, empiricism and utilitarianism, together with a receptive but highly modified version of Greek *eudaimonism*, neo-Kantianism and Hegelianism.

iv

The third domain of Green's legacy is the one which has had the most enduring impact. This is politics. The central category of Green's political philosophy is "citizenship". Citizenship implied a consciousness of the ends of human life as embodied within the institutional structures of the modern state, in other words, a consciousness of the *common good*. The state was seen as the organised body within which this consciousness functions. For Green, society and its institutional structures were the means to individual self-realization. Social institutions were therefore justified only to the extent that they furthered the self-realisation of individuals. The citizen, for Green, was not simply the passive recipient of rights, but rather an active self-realizing being. Green viewed all political concepts from this standpoint. Rights, obligations, property or freedom were devices to enable all citizens to realise their powers and abilities. The nub of Green's vision of politics was that of providing an "enabling state". This vision of the state created a setting for later developments of the welfare state in twentieth century Britain.

It would be no exaggeration to say that the majority of the senior public servants who worked on and supported the early twentieth century British welfare state reforms between 1906 and 1914, for example, W.H. Beveridge, R.B. Morant, Llewellyn Smith, Ernest Aves, W.J. Braithwaite, J.A. Spender, R.H. Tawney and Clement Atlee were profoundly influenced by the culture of civic idealism and social duty initially inspired by Green. Thus, if there is one important intellectual political bequest from Green, it is an optimistic ethical theory of citizenship and the state, dedicated to the promotion of a worthwhile life for all citizens.

In practical political terms Green, following John Bright, was an enthusiastic supporter of the extension of the franchise. He was a member of the Oxford Reform League which backed the national franchise campaigns before the 1867 Reform Bill. He also worked in his local Liberal party organisation and in 1875 was elected as a Liberal member to Oxford Town Council.

Green was also closely associated with the temperance movement, joining the United Kingdom Alliance in 1872 and publicly committing himself to teetotalism.[16] His personal interest in this issue included setting up a coffee tavern in St. Clements, Oxford in 1875. Apart from the fact that his brother suffered from severe alcoholism, it is also important to note that, even after the 1874 Licensing Act, child and adult drunkenness was rife in industrial and agricultural areas of Britain. Green saw intemperance as part of a connected pattern of inequality and poverty, characteristic of a policy of *laissez-faire* liberalism. His views on temperance were thus consistent with his

---

[16] He was also President of the Oxford Temperance Alliance, and Treasurer to the Oxford Diocesan Branch of the Church of England Temperance Society, and President of the Oxfordshire Band of Hope and Temperance Union from 1876.

more general political philosophy. Alcohol was yet another potential impediment to the citizen's development.[17]

V

The fourth aspect of Green's legacy lay in the sphere of education. Green saw education as the great social leveller in society, delivering equal opportunities, if not equal outcomes. The role of education was part of the more general "enabling role" of the state. Education was also viewed as an intrinsic part of the philosophical enterprise. It linked up with an understanding of human nature and its potential for development. It was premised on a radical egalitarian principle which had no truck with any class or status differentiation; conversely, it was orientated to an equality of opportunity for all citizens. The aim was therefore to establish the secure groundwork for the development of ethical citizenship. Green was impatient with individualistic liberal theories which tried to play down the role of the state. It was rather the positive duty of the state to establish a national education system, from primary level to university level, which, at many points, should be legally compulsory. Overall, Green's theory offered an ethical vision of education. His ideas on a "ladder of learning" for all citizens, from primary to university level, directly influenced both R.B. Haldane and H.A.L. Fisher and, indirectly, early twentieth century British education policy.

In practical terms, Green in 1864 was appointed an assistant-commissioner in the Midlands to the Schools Inquiry Commission chaired by Lord Taunton. His main responsibility, until 1866, was to inspect the endowed schools of Warwickshire and Staffordshire and later Buckingham, Leicester and Northampton. The final report of the commission, with Green's contribution, was published in 1868. The Endowed Schools Act of 1869, however, nowhere lived up to Green's vision for the Idealist reconstitution of society through national education. After his commission work, Green was elected as a teacher's representative on the governing body of King Edward's School in Birmingham. Contrary to many contemporaneous classical liberals, Green believed in making education both

---

[17] Green favoured the "local option" policy, which entailed local control on the sale of alcohol. In 1873, he came into open dispute with the Liberal Chancellor of the Exchequer, Sir William Harcourt, over the latter's opposition to tighter regulation on alcohol.

universal and legally compulsory. He argued this latter point from the early 1870s and it was finally legislated by the Liberals in 1880. Green argued that compulsion did not entail any encroachment on the liberties of parents. On the contrary, to compel parents to educate their children removed an obstacle to the effective growth of the capacity in the next generation to exercise their rights and freedoms as citizens. Green thus argued for a national approach to education which would remove powers from the church and local school boards and establish responsibilities at the level of county school boards.

Green deplored the elitism of universities of the time and their separation from local communities. He argued robustly for extending access to higher education to poorer students. With the support of Jowett, Balliol Hall - an annex to the main Oxford college - was provided for students with financial difficulties. Green presided over the hall. He was also a keen supporter of the fledgling University Extension Movement, which began in the 1870s, as well as women's university education. Green's authoritative philosophical advocacy had a powerful effect on a number of crucial public figures involved in the restructuring of British education in the early twentieth century, certainly up to the 1920s. Key civil servants such as Arthur Acland, R.B. Morant, M.T. Sadler, Llewellyn Smith, amongst others, were all deeply influenced by his arguments.

One final educational movement, which derived directly from Green, was the idea university settlements. The first of these – Toynbee Hall in Whitechapel - was founded in memory of Green's student Arnold Toynbee. Another early settlement the Passmore Edwards Settlement, was founded by Mrs Humphrey Ward in 1896. Mrs Ward's novel *Robert Elsmere* (1907) contains a thinly disguised heroic portrait of Green as the key character, Professor Grey. Settlements were designed not just for working class education, as such, but also to re-educate university students through their participation in the duties of mutual citizenship.

Conclusion

Green is unique within the British Idealist school.[18] Although not an easy writer, Green had an immensely positive effect on generations of students,

---

[18] See David Boucher and Andrew Vincent, *British Idealism: A Guide to the Perplexed* (London: Continuum Press, 2012).

including many future academics, churchmen, politicians and public servants, for example, men such as Herbert Asquith, Edward Grey, Alfred Milner, Arthur Acland, A.C. Bradley, Arnold Toynbee, Bernard Bosanquet, R.L. Nettleship, Charles Gore and Henry Scott Holland. As R.G. Collingwood noted famously in his *Autobiography* (1939), Green's major effect was to send out into public life "a stream of ex-pupils who carried with them the conviction that philosophy ... was an important thing, and their vocation was to put it into practice .... Through this effect on the minds of its pupils, the philosophy of Green's school might be found, from 1880 to about 1910, penetrating and fertilizing every part of the national life."[19] After Green's death, in 1882, he also left a powerful legacy, and, in part mythology, concerning his achievements, which carried through well into the early twentieth century.

---

[19] R.G. Collingwood, *An Autobiography* (Oxford: Oxford University Press, 1939), p.17.

Sidgwick and Hare

A C Grayling

Henry Sidgwick

The most direct line of connection between Henry Sidgwick and R. M. Hare, two of the most salient names in the last two centuries of English ethical thought, lies in this remark by Sidgwick in his classic

The Methods of Ethics (1874)[1]: "I have thought that the predominance in the minds of moralists of a desire to edify has impeded the real progress of ethical science: and that this would be benefited by an application to it of the same disinterested curiosity to which we chiefly owe the great discoveries of physics. It is in this spirit that I have endeavoured to compose the present work: and with this view I have desired to concentrate the reader's attention, from first to last not on the practical results to which our methods lead, but on the methods themselves" (*MoE* Introduction).

Such was the influence of Sidgwick on philosophical debate about ethics thereafter, that when R. M. Hare published his *Language of Morals* in 1952 he was able to say that it is not the duty of the moral philosopher to say what is good and bad, and how people ought to live, but only to examine the logic of moral statements, and the concepts deployed in making them.

Coming so few years after one of the greatest moral outrages in the history of humankind – the Holocaust of European Jewry – and the general situation in a world torn apart by war; coming even as the ruins created by human conflict still smoked, and the rubble lay strewn everywhere, and humankind continued to reel from the trauma; coming even as the echoes of bomb explosions and the screams of the dying had not quite faded from contemporary ears – this remark might seem like a despicable betrayal of the ethical duty once so simply and profoundly imposed by Socrates: to consider life, and on that basis to answer the question, "What sort of people should we be?"

It happens that I have some sympathy with the view that moral philosophy, at least in the analytic tradition, has indeed failed in this respect. But that was not Sidgwick's intention, and it cannot have been Hare's either, for he had suffered captivity by the Japanese during the war after the fall of Singapore in 1942, and knew first hand what urgency attached to the question of how one should live – especially when it involved knowing how to endure, and how not to fail in moral life when severe inducements to do so present themselves.

---

[1] All references to *The Methods of Ethics* are to the 7th edition 1907; there is a Hackett reprint with an introduction by John Rawls 1981.

R M Hare

This can be appreciated by noting how the passage just cited from Sidgwick continues. He wrote, "I have wished to put aside temporarily the urgent need which we all feel of finding and adopting the true method of determining what we ought to do; and to consider simply what conclusions will be rationally reached if we start with certain ethical premises, and with what degree of certainty and precision" (*MoE* p. vi). And indeed he later wrote directly about questions of practical ethics. Those who took the even more austere view that ethics is not a normative pursuit, that moral philosophers are not experts in how people should behave, were Sidgwick's successors only in following the first point quoted. But they did it for the reason he gave: that ethics must benefit from the application of "the same disinterested curiosity to which we chiefly owe the great discoveries of physics."

So, both Sidgwick and Hare had a point. Without a thorough examination of the methods and concepts of ethical thought, the normative task of saying how we should live and what sort of people we should be cannot be well done. It was to this task that Sidgwick devoted his classic study, and to which Hare devoted all his best philosophical endeavours likewise.

Sidgwick's *Methods of Ethics* is the first truly modern study of ethical concepts and theories. The book went through seven editions in all, revisions for the last edition being completed after his death and appearing in 1907. By a "method of ethics" Sidgwick meant "any rational procedure by which we determine what individual human beings "ought" – or what it is "right" for them – to do" (*MoE* p. 1.) The three methods of ethics he discusses are egoism, utilitarianism, and intuitionism, and his aim in examining them can be described as trying to find a way of reconciling what is right in each with what is right in the others. All three views were in full play in the debates about morality in the century up to and including Sidgwick's time, and they were related to the unsettled state of religious debate in the same period, in ways which were of crucial personal importance to Sidgwick himself.

Each of the "methods of ethics" discussed by Sidgwick is more complex than the following summary characterisations suggests. Egoism is the view that right actions are those that tend to the agent's good, where the good is identified with happiness. Utilitarianism is the view that right actions are those promote the greatest good for the greatest number. Intuitionism is the view that right actions are those that conform to "precepts or principles of Duty, intuitively known to be unconditionally binding" (*MoE* p. 3).

It turns out that although Sidgwick was aiming to give a dispassionate analysis of what is at stake in each of these views, he does indeed take sides in *Methods of Ethics*. As he came to see it, there is no conflict between utilitarianism and intuitionism, because the former rests on intuitively recognizable ethical principles in very much the way that the latter claims. The opposition, rather, is between these views on the one hand, and egoism on the other, for the obvious reason that there can be and often are conflicts between what is in one's own interest and what one can know intuitively to promote a general good. When the conflict is irresolvable it gives rise to what Sidgwick called "the Dualism of Practical Reason."

The serious problem thus posed is what led Sidgwick to think that the only way to resolve the conflict is to come down on one side of it, this side being a utilitarianism whose fundamental principles are intuitable. But he further thought that such utilitarianism requires that there be the possibility of compensation for sufferings experienced and sanctions for wrongs committed, which he thought could only realistically happen in a posthumous state, which – obviously – requires that personal individuality should survive bodily death. This has been suggested, very plausibly, as the motivation for something that surprises many when they come to learn more about Sidgwick after first encountering his masterpiece of ethical enquiry – namely, his great interest in spiritualism and psychical research.

In a letter to a friend written in January 1870 he wrote that the solution to the problem of ethics had to lie in one or other of "the evidence supplied by Spiritualism" or "religious grounds" or "the Postulate of Immortality." He there adds that his own inclination is to the last of these three (he described himself as having an "inherited disposition" to believe this, and thought that so many shared this view that it almost possessed "the authority of a belief of Common Sense").[2] This remark by itself does not suggest why he distinguishes between "the evidence of Spiritualism" and the concept of immortality, which have a natural enough connection, though Spiritualism requires only survival of bodily death, not immortality as such; temporary survival would suffice for its phenomena. Almost all religions suppose posthumous forms of existence, but Sidgwick is right to think that neither spiritualism nor personal immortality have to have religious implications.

But Sidgwick was too scrupulous a thinker to rest content with what it would have been convenient to think as a resolution to ethical problems. Over the two decades following the writing of the 1870 remarks just quoted, he came reluctantly to the view that all efforts to establish the existence of an afterlife had failed. Although he said that he was determined to carry on searching for conclusive evidence one way or the other, the routes to doing

---

[2] Gaud, Alan, 'Henry Sidgwick, Theism and Psychical Research' (2009) http://www.henrysidgwick.com/4th-paper.1st.congress.cat.eng.html

so – empirical, religious, and rational – pointed to the dismaying (for him) conclusion that there is no survival of death. This plunged him into serious gloom, and he even wondered whether he could continue teaching moral philosophy if it is nothing more than a "chaos" in which the "Dualism of Practical Reason" is forever irreducible.[3] Like so many – but not all – of his forebears and contemporaries he seemed not to be able to grasp that an entirely secular basis for morality can provide a rich impulse to seek and to live lives that are good, responsible, continent, benevolent and fulfilling. The attraction of the view that self-interest can only be opposed by what, ultimately and even if deeply covert in formulation, is the potential exercise of coercive power – the threat of punishment, which is actually no ground for morality at all, but only for prudence – seems to have been a thorn on which Sidgwick's otherwise scrupulous intellect remained permanently snagged.

As the foregoing implies, a religious basis for morality was not available to Sidgwick, because he had come to think that the most he could subscribe to in the way of theology was a general theism, a belief that there is some overarching principle of good in the universe. But he could not be a Christian, and much of his thinking as of his personal history turns on his painful disengagement from the religious commitments of his earlier years.

Henry Sidgwick was born in 1838, the son of a Church of England clergyman who was himself the son of a well-to-do North of England cotton manufacturer. Sidgwick's father was educated at Trinity College, Cambridge, and a few years after ordination was appointed headmaster of a grammar school in Skipton, Yorkshire. He died when Sidgwick was just three years of age, leaving his widow with four children to look after. In 1852 Sidgwick commenced at Rugby School, leaving in 1855 for his father's old college at Cambridge. There he had an outstanding undergraduate career, which culminated in his being elected to a Fellowship at Trinity in 1859; and there he remained for the rest of his life.

It is worth noting that when Sidgwick was at Rugby the headmaster was E. M. Goulburn, a rather speaking surname, since he was the author of a defence of the Christian doctrine of eternal damnation for unsaved sinners. This implies a certain cold orthodoxy in the religious life of the school,

---

[3] Sidgwick A. & E. M., *Henry Sidgwick A Memoir* pp. 472-3.

introduced to counter any lingering influence of the famous Dr Arnold, which by then had come to be viewed by increasingly-dominant Evangelicals as too liberal. But perhaps the greater influence at that stage in Sidgwick's religious development was E. W. Benson, in later life Archbishop of Canterbury, who lived with the Sidgwicks in Rugby and married one of his sisters. Benson was a high-minded moralist although neither so narrow nor so much of an enthusiast in his theology as some of his contemporaries. But like Goulburn, Benson was not prepared for the challenges to Christianity then beginning to emerge, and did not prepare his charges for them either. Sidgwick encountered these challenges at Cambridge, and they proved fatal to such orthodoxy as he had acquired at home and school.

The challenges came variously from the scholarship of Strauss and Renan on the life of Jesus, from the ideas of August Comte and John Stuart Mill, from Darwin and the theory of evolution, from such modernisers in theology as "the Seven Against Christ" (the authors of the famous *Essays and Reviews* 1860, published just a year after *The Origin of Species*), and from Sidgwick's own contemporaries at Cambridge, not least when he was invited to join the semi-secret intellectual society called the "Apostles," where discussion was encouraged to be utterly frank, engaging in (as Sidgwick put it) "the pursuit of truth with absolute devotion and unreserve."

It is no surprise that this heady mixture of ideas and debate should act as it did on so careful a mind as Sidgwick possessed. When he was elected to his Fellowship at Trinity he had to subscribe the Thirty Nine Articles of the Church of England. It was not long before he began to feel uncomfortable about his commitment to those articles, and not long again – a mere decade – before he felt it was dishonest to hold his Fellowship on the basis of them, given that he could no longer in conscience subscribe to them. He resigned his Fellowship in 1869, but was immediately appointed to a College Lectureship, and resumed his Fellowship when the legal requirement for subscription to the Articles was at last abolished. In 1883 he became Knightbridge Professor of Moral Philosophy, the university's principal philosophical chair.

Sidgwick began his academic career as a teacher of classics, migrating to philosophy as the Moral Science Tripos evolved into a degree subject. His interests were wide. In addition to ethics he lectured on the theory of knowledge, metaphysics, political theory, law and legal theory. Outside these academic fields he was a lover of poetry, for which he had a prodigious memory, and Shakespeare. He was a considerable linguist, adding German, Arabic and Hebrew to his knowledge of the classical languages. And he was deeply interested in providing opportunities for higher education for women; perhaps his single greatest achievement other than writing *The Methods of Ethics* was the founding of Newnham College, the first women's college at Cambridge. In 1876 he had married Eleanor Balfour, sister of the Arthur Balfour who later became Prime Minister. She served as Newnham's second principal, and Sidgwick lived with her at Newnham, helping with the teaching of the women students.

The interest, already mentioned, in spiritualism and psychic phenomena absorbed a great deal of Sidgwick's time also. The Society for Psychical Research (SPR) was founded in 1882 with him as its first President. He served in this capacity for many years, donating money to it, participating in research on mediums and hauntings, and contributing many articles to its journals. As we have seen, his intense interest in phenomena that could indicate individual survival of bodily death was related to his quest for an ethical theory, and the failure of the SPR's endeavours to find such evidence was for him a great disappointment.

But long before the foundation of the SPR and Sidgwick's disappointment in the outcome of its efforts, he had ceased to be Christian, adopting instead a view he described as Rationalism which, although a vaguely theistic one, laid emphasis on the idea that the moral sense of mankind evolves on the basis of common sense and reason, and the shared experience of humankind. In an article for the *Pall Mall Gazette* in 1870 he wrote, "the Rationalist holds that the theology of the Bible has, and always will have, a unique interest for mankind, but unique only as the interest of Greek philosophy is unique, because it is the fountain from which the main stream of thought upon the subject is derived…But he holds that no explanation, even of these truths by the Biblical writers, is to be regarded as authoritative; that the process of development which the Historical Scripturalist traces between the earlier and later of them has continued since, and will continue, and that we cannot forecast its limits; and that even where the doctrine of the Bible, taken as a whole, is clear an appeal lies always open to the common sense, common reason, and combined experience of the religious portion of mankind…I incline myself to the view that I have termed Rationalism, and conceive that the thought of civilized Europe is moving rapidly in its direction, and that it must inevitably spread and prevail." As he himself put it, this process amounted to a "revolution."

One immediate consequence of allowing appeal to the formidable tribunals of common sense, experience and reason over the claims of revelation is – for example – that one cannot accept as true the stories of miracles in the Bible; and if they are not to be believed, then the theology they are alleged to support cannot be accepted. This was one of the chief sources of Sidgwick's own rejection of the Christian faith.[4]

The joint result of Sidgwick's struggles with religion and contemplation of ethics is distilled in *The Methods of Ethic,* a work he continued to revise, rearrange and expand throughout his life. His own account of the evolution of his thought, written shortly before his death, is an excellent summary of it. It occurs in notes for a lecture that he was composing at the time that preparations were in hand for the 6th edition of his masterwork. He wrote that the first ethical system he adhered to was Mill's utilitarianism – an interesting fact, given that utilitarianism only began to be really influential after the 1861 publication of Mill's classic eponymous text, at the time that Sidgwick was a young don. In Mill's views Sidgwick says that he "found relief from the external and arbitrary pressure of moral rules which I had been educated to obey, and which presented themselves to me as to some extent doubtful and confused; and sometimes, even when clear, as merely dogmatic, unreasoned, incoherent" (*MoE* p. xvii). His adoption of Mill's point of view was strengthened by opposition to the attack on utilitarianism mounted by William Whewell, then professor at Cambridge, whom Sidgwick of necessity heard lecture; and in any case Whewell's anti-utilitarian *Elements of Morality* was a prescribed text at Trinity. Whewell was an emphatic supporter of the view propounded by another Cambridge don, Alan Sedgwick (sic; no connection to Sidgwick) that, as J. B. Schneewind reports it, "all branches of learning [at Cambridge] could and should be subservient to the religious improvement of [the] students."[5] Sidgwick says of Whewell's book that he learned from it that "Intuitional moralists were hopelessly loose (as compared to mathematicians) in their definitions and axioms" (*MoE* p. xvii).

---

[4] See Broad C. D. *Religion, Philosophy and Psychical Research* 1953, p. 108 quoted Gauld.
[5] Schneewind J. B. *Sidgwick's Ethics and Victorian Moral Philosophy* Oxford 1977 p. 89. This excellent book is indispensable to any student of Sidgwick's life, times and thought.

But after a time Sidgwick became conscious of two conflicting aspects to Mill's views, one saying that everyone seeks his own happiness and another saying that people ought to promote the general happiness. This tension between Self-Interest and Duty caused him deep concern. This set him on the path of research that led to *The Methods of Ethics*.

The result of that research "was that I concluded that no complete solution of the conflict between my happiness and the general happiness was possible on the basis of mundane experience" (*MoE* p. xviii). It was a conclusion he only "slowly and reluctantly accepted," and it prompted in its turn a search for the ground on which a choice was to be made between them (*MoE* ibid). That search resulted in acceptance of the need for "a fundamental ethical intuition" which, Sidgwick says, he was forced to recognize "despite my early aversion to Intuitional Ethics, derived from the study of Whewell, and in spite of my attitude of discipleship to Mill" (*MoE* ibid).

The journey that took Sidgwick to this conclusion encompassed the study of Kant and Butler, and much reflection on what he called Common Sense Morality, keeping him true to his regulative principle that ethical enquiry should respect what is practical and actual and not only what is ideal. In line with this he was able to draw a conclusion that is a classical statement of "hedonistic utilitarianism": that the ultimate good is pleasure, and that the more that pleasure outweighs pain in one's experience, the better one's life is.[6] The important point is that pleasure in Sidgwick's view is of course not merely sensual or ego-directed; there is pleasure in virtuous action, in freedom from guilt and remorse, in promoting the pleasure of others, and in conforming to moral impulses with which Common Sense equips everyone (*MoE* p. 164). These rest on the intuition that determines which side of the fault-line between Interest and Duty one's choices are to lie.

Richard Mervyn Hare was also a utilitarian, although in the book that made him famous, *The Language of Morals,* utilitarianism was a minor theme merely, and his commitment to that view only emerged in fullest form in later work. In order better to grasp the major outlines of his thought, one does well to read his later book *Moral Thinking: Its Levels, Methods and Point* (1981).

---

[6] See the fine discussion of Sidgwick's views by Crisp, Roger 'Sidgwick's Hedonism' (2009) http://www.henrysidgwick.com/3rd-paper.1st.congress.cat.eng.html

When Hare wrote *The Language of Morals* the prevailing view in moral philosophy was a form of emotivism, the theory that moral judgments are disguised statements of subjective preference on the part of those making them. Hare's book was published in 1952, at the very height of the influence of Wittgenstein and the school of "Ordinary Language Philosophy" of which J. L. Austen was the formidable leading light in Oxford, where Hare was teaching. Accordingly Hare's views had the power of much originality in them, for he argued that moral assertions are not expressions of attitude but prescriptions for action, which moreover are universalisable – that is, hold validly for anyone anywhere in the same kind of circumstances as one acting on them in a given case. The universalisability of prescriptions underpins their rationality. The later commitment to utilitarianism Hare saw as following from the two features of prescriptivity and universalisability.

Hare's views invited much criticism and debate, inevitable in so fine-tooth-combing an intellectual environment as recent and contemporary philosophy constitutes, and he was a robust defender of his views, not hesitating to repeat them often in subsequent papers and books in order to deal with what he took to be mainly misunderstandings rather than disagreements. But there is no question that his contribution to moral philosophy was enormous; it is not possible to study the subject today without including his ideas in the discussion, and as a teacher at Balliol College he superintended the philosophical education of some the twentieth century's leading philosophical minds, among them Bernard Williams and Peter Singer.

Hare was born in Somerset in 1919, and was educated at Rugby School and then Balliol College Oxford. Despite a desire to be a pacifist he enlisted in the Royal Artillery when the Second World War broke out. He was among those captured when Singapore fell to the Japanese in 1942, and spent the remainder of the war as their prisoner. He was known to remark that he knew what it was like to be a Burmese coolie "because he had actually been one"; yet despite his experiences as a PoW of the Japanese, who were not signatories to the Geneva Conventions on treatment of prisoners of war and were notably harsh gaolers as a result, he never bore them any grudges, and was said to have been pleased by the fact that his works were held in high reputation in Japan.

The experience of imprisonment did however inspire his philosophical thinking in the sense that he wished – so one of his obituarists claimed he said – to develop an ethics that would sustain individuals even in the harshest circumstances.[7]

Hare completed his degree at Oxford on returning from the East, and was immediately made a Fellow and Tutor of Balliol, where he remained until becoming White's Professor of Moral Philosophy and a Fellow of Corpus Christi College in 1966. True to the times in which he lived, Hare was a professional philosopher first and foremost, a teacher and writer whose adumbration of an original view was followed by its development, application and defence in the course of the characteristic debates that taking a distinctive position in recent and contemporary philosophy invites. One of the respects in which he was like Sidgwick (with whom, nevertheless, he disagreed on a number of points, not least on the reliability of common sense intuitions in ethics) was that clarity and scrupulous thinking are essential to making progress in philosophical thinking.

One way of describing Hare's moral philosophy is to say that it is a combination of Kant's universalisability criterion – the criterion that distinguishes a truly moral judgment, a *categorical* one, from a merely prudential or hypothetical one - with a version of utilitarianism known as "preference utilitarianism." Hare's argument is that the logic of moral language is such that judgments about what ought to be done, or what it is right to do, by their nature apply to anyone who is in the kind of circumstances where such a judgment is appropriate, and they take precedence over any other maxim or prescription enjoining an alternative course of action. This is true no matter to whom the judgment applies. Assenting to the proposition that such-and-such is what ought to be done in the case is to state a preference that it be done. However, although most people have generally similar preferences about what is the right thing to do in the typical circumstances of life, there is also a need for critical reflection to help in cases where differences in experience, intelligence, and power of action make it difficult for a decision to be reached. This is where intuitive and general thinking about principles has to be supplemented with critical thinking.

---

[7] This quotation is sourced to *The Independent* obituary on the occasion of Hare's death in 2002.

It is certain that these two net contributors to ethics owe something particular to the school they both attended; how could it be otherwise? It is of course hard to disengage positive from negative influences, and influences of educational ethos from the accidents of friendship, historical circumstances and personality. But it is an interesting consideration that as they thought and wrote, both these major figures of English moral philosophy might have reflected upon something related to their Warwickshire school and the people they knew there, whether teachers or fellow-students. One day, perhaps, someone might make a study of the social and intellectual ecology surrounding the development of our culture's greater contributors, to see what if anything might be learned. If there are such lessons, we would all willingly apply them, to ensure more Sidgwicks and Hares to help continue the conversation of mankind on the nature of the good and the right in life.

R. H. Tawney: The Making of a Christian socialist

Jay Winter

R.H. Tawney was the voice of Christian socialism in Britain in the first half of the twentieth century. He was the inspiration for a generation at war with the religion of inequality in British life, and he pointed the way for men and women who shared his Anglican faith and other faiths and who led the struggle in other domains, in particular, the war against Apartheid and the anti-nuclear movement after 1950.

Born in 1880 in imperial India, Tawney was the son of a Sanskrit scholar, Principal of Presidency College in Calcutta, at which school he received his early education. Thereafter, he returned to England and followed the scholar's path from Rugby to Balliol. Tawney never wrote about India, though he took an active interest in China's rural development. Neither Asia nor empire was the focus of his political work.

Instead he applied his moral commitments, his energy, his intelligence, and his charisma to the problem of social and economic inequality at home. After Oxford, he lived in the East End of London, at Toynbee Hall, an experiment in finding ways for well-educated men and women to cross the boundaries of social class, primarily through education. William Beveridge and Clement Attlee were among his cohort of Oxford men who decided to take up residence there, in the midst of the poor living at the heart of the richest city in the world. The fruits of empire lay behind British prosperity, but the global reach of British capitalism was not the primary interest of these young reformers; the injustices evident within England itself offered them plenty of scope for action.

From Toynbee Hall in East London, in the midst of Irish and Eastern European Jewish immigrants, they looked the inequalities of social class squarely in the face. Life expectancy for men in early Edwardian England was about 47 years, or roughly the same level reached by India in 1970. Infant mortality rates – a good indicator of poverty – stood at 140 deaths before age one to 1000 children born in England. East End statistics were even worse. Life chances were a lottery of birth, and working-class children especially in the East End of London got the short end of the stick from the moment they were born. Children born into professional families had twice the life expectancy at birth as children born in working-class families. Even though this indicator fell rapidly in the twentieth century, the ratio between infant mortality in professional families and in the families of manual labourers remained constant. Inequality was both absolute and relative, evidently built into the structure of British society and institutions. Where better than Toynbee Hall in Whitechapel to see what inequality looked like in 1903?

To a Christian like Tawney, inequality was so deeply ingrained in British language and culture that it constituted virtually a religion, a form of accounting for the way the world worked, and in that respect, what he termed the religion of inequality was incompatible with his Christian beliefs. We do not know if his Anglican convictions were a matter of his early years in India, or of his schooling at Rugby and later at Balliol. William Temple, later Archbishop of Canterbury, born in 1881, a year after Tawney, was his contemporary at Rugby and Balliol, and the friendship between the two men lasted a lifetime. What is clear is that Tawney's belief in God was firm from his early years and that he maintained a sense of mission in this world as a test of his beliefs.

At Toynbee Hall he joined others in launching the Workers' Educational Association, an institution dedicated to breaking the monopoly the middle and upper classes had on higher education in England. By inviting men and women whose working lives had cut short their education to join university-trained teachers in university level courses, the WEA was a practical test of the power of education to blur class distinctions. It was not, as some critics have suggested, a plan to co-opt working-class men and women into a national culture,[1] but to create a different kind of national culture forged by educational work done together.

Solidarity and fellowship were its two watchwords, and a commitment to both was what Tawney, alongside Temple and others, gave to the WEA. The Christian character of this project and of his general outlook before the war is evident in the diary or Commonplace Book he kept from 1910-14. It is not clear what moved him to keep this spiritual diary. He married in 1909 to Jeannette Beveridge, sister of William Beveridge, but neither expressed religious convictions of any similar kind. Perhaps he used these entries to find out what he felt about the overlap between social and sacred matters; perhaps he used them to mull over matters he could not exchange with his wife or his friends. Whatever the origins, this remarkable diary tells us much about Tawney the Christian socialist on the eve of the Great War.[2]

Tawney's work in the WEA was an expression of his belief that all men should "think of knowledge, like religion, as transcending all differences of class, and wealth", since "in the eye of learning as in the eye of God, all men

---

[1] Roger Fieldhouse, 'Conformity and contradiction in English responsible body adult education, 1925-1950', *Studies in the Education of Adults*, 17 (October 1985), p. 123.
[2] J.M. Winter and D.M. Joslin (eds), *R.H. Tawney's Commonplace Book* (Cambridge: Cambridge University Press, 1972). Hereafter cited as 'Commonplace Book'.

are equal because all are infinitely small".³ English education was corrupt to the extent that it was infused by the values of contemporary society, which is to say, the values of capitalist materialism. "To sell education for money is the next thing to selling the gifts of God for money", and just as intolerable, in Tawney's view.⁴

His Christian convictions gave both his teaching and his scholarship their particular flavour. He dedicated his first book in historical scholarship, *The Agrarian problem in the sixteenth century*, to William Temple, and to the founder of the WEA, Alfred Mansbridge. He then went on to acknowledge that "the friendly smitings of weavers, potters, miners, and engineers" in his WEA classes, "have taught me much about problems of political and economic science which cannot easily be learned from books". In terms of his thought on contemporary society, his sense of indebtedness was even more striking. "My views, such as they are", he wrote before the Great War, "have been formed by intercourse with working people".⁵

Those views were Christian socialist, in the sense that he used Christian language to describe what he saw as a growing consciousness among working people as to the glaring contradiction between the social and economic organization of capitalist industry and what ordinary people took to be morally right. This was the source, he believed, of the labour unrest of 1910-12, which had both a material and a moral character. Poverty in the midst of great wealth was a moral outrage "on that which is sacred in man".⁶ Wage slavery – meaning the workings of a labour market offering pitiful wages and insecurity to millions of unskilled labourers – fuelled the "moral abhorrence" of men and women on strike just as much as chattel slavery had done. "It is in economic affairs", he believed, that "the objective order is most violently in contradiction to men's conception of right".⁷

Underlying his early political thought is his religious faith, his sense of the existence of God as what he termed

---

³ Commonplace Book, 26 Oct. 2012.
⁴ Commonplace Book, 26 Oct. 1912.
⁵ Notes for a lecture in late 1912 or early 1913, Tawney papers, London School of Economics.
⁶ Commonplace Book. 10 June 1912.
⁷ Tawney, 'An Experiment in democratic education', *Political Quarterly* (May 1914), p. 4.

"a fact of experience, by which I mean that consciousness of contact with a personality, or with a source of right and emotion,... infinitely more immediate than reflection on an absent but existing person, and analogous to the consciousness of the presence of the person in the same room as oneself, whom one is not at the moment looking at, and with whom one communicates nonetheless easily on that account."

Social conflict arose, in Tawney's view, when men saw oppression in the same way as they saw sin, as a violation of moral standards which applied to groups as well as to individuals. His model of social conflict is deeply Protestant: "Just as the individual suffers", he wrote, citing Fox and Bunyan, "when his habits of conduct are in contradiction to his conscience within him, so society suffers when its objective institutions outrage the best ideals of the age".[8]

Tawney was perfectly prepared to admit – at least to his Commonplace Book – that his standard of both personal and social behaviour was "really a transcendental, religious or mystical one". He also stated clearly that his sense of social conduct arose out of his religious beliefs. His faith compelled him to accept personal guilt, as a man of privilege – Rugby and Balliol -- for the injustices and failures of his society. Tawney's sense of ethical conflict in society was inseparable from his own very intense feeling of sin, the belief "that what goodness we have reached is a house built on piles driven into black slime and always slipping down into it unless we are building day and night".[9] This consciousness of sin made his theory of conflict a limited one; what Kant termed the crooked tree of humanity could never point to utopia.

And yet this form of Christian socialism could point to the end of the sway of capitalism and inequality through stripping from them their aura as natural and inevitable forms of social organization. Reforms would then follow. Strikes and administrative and legal reform were necessary, but they were less important to Tawney than a kind of moral rearmament. The crucial task for socialists in pre-war England, he noted, was to "deepen our individual sense of sin" and to "objectify our morality".[10]

---

[8] Commonplace Book, 6 May 2012.
[9] Commonplace Book, 30 June 1912.
[10] Commonplace Book, 6 May 1912.

Wartime

The same sense of moral obligation led Tawney to volunteer for the British army in November 1914 and to serve in the ranks in the Manchester Regiment. He approached his military service as a matter of conscience, accepting the then overwhelmingly popular view that the Allied resistance to German aggression in Belgium and France was a moral cause.

He was among the 40,000 British soldiers wounded on the first day of the Battle of the Somme on 1 July 1916. Hit in the side, he spent a day that felt like eternity waiting for stretcher bearers to arrive. They did, but from then onward, Tawney never forgot what he saw as his experience of the cross.

He was totally aware that he was one of the killers as well as one of the victims of the war. To him, the fact that he hit the enemy with his rifle fire was no matter for celebration. He felt, he wrote shortly afterwards, like a merry mischievous ape tearing up the image of God. Convalescence took time, first at the home of the Bishop of Oxford, Charles Gore, and then at his old College, Balliol, where he spent a year as a Fellow to collect his thoughts after the war and plot his future course of action.

In 1918 he stood unsuccessfully as a Labour party candidate for Rochdale, and then turned towards other forms of service to the Labour movement. In 1919, he served as a member of the Royal Commission on the Coal Mines, nominated by the Miners Federation of Great Britain, alongside Beatrice and Sidney Webb. This body recommended nationalization, but Lloyd George cleverly waved away its conclusions since the commissioners did not agree on the form the new coal industry would take. The result was a 27-year delay in turning the mines into a public asset and a public service.

In the same year, he accepted a post as Reader in Economic History at the London School of Economics, his academic home until retirement in 1949. Named to a chair in LSE in 1931, he helped shape the subject as a branch of moral philosophy. He also wrote what we would now term tracts for the times, essays in contemporary political economy with wide appeal to the rank and file of the Labour movement. The point of view he developed in these works is still alive today.

Let us deal first with his contribution to the academic field of economic history. In the first phase of his work, started with his book *The Agrarian problem in the sixteenth century,* and encompassed as well his 1925 introduction to Thomas Wilson's *Discourse on usury* (1569), and his most celebrated historical study *Religion and the rise of capitalism* (1926). In these works, Tawney defined economic history as the study of the resistance of groups and individuals to the imposition on them of capitalist modes of thought and behavior. In the 1930s, in the second phase of his academic work, in the shadow of the world economic crisis and the onward march of fascism, Tawney wrote about the economic roots of political dominance, political collapse and revolution. This was more a change of emphasis and sources rather than a change of beliefs. In this period and during the Second World War he developed an interpretation of the links between land-holding and political power in the sixteenth and seventeenth centuries which had what may be termed not a Marxist but a *Marxisant* flavor to it.

His most celebrated work shows the impact of his Anglican faith, and his ongoing discussions with other Anglicans, led by Bishop Temple of Manchester, about the social responsibility of the Church. Tawney was shrewd enough to aim at converting Christians into socialism, rather than converting socialists to Christianity.

In his pre-war commonplace book, he wondered "if Puritanism produced any special attitude to economic matters".[11] It is apparent that he was unaware of Max Weber's essay on "The Protestant ethic and the spirit of capitalism", published seven years before. In 1922 he was asked to give the Scott Holland lectures at King's College, London on some aspect of "the religion of the Incarnation in its bearing on the social and economic life of man". The ideas he expressed there were developed in his 1925 edition of Thomas Wilson's *Discourse on Usury.* There he showed how widespread was condemnation of the burgeoning economic system we now call capitalism not as "the crudities of a young and brilliant civilization, but the collapse of public morality in a welter of disorderly appetites".[12]

This subject was at the heart of his *Religion and the Rise of Capitalism,* published a year later. He showed the vigorous contestation of economic individualism – what is today termed rational choice – within Calvinist

---

[11] Commonplace Book, 16 Sept. 1912.
[12] *A Discourse on Usury*, p. 16.

thought itself. Calvin, and all those whose ideas flowed out of his, went through a process of modulating their views that economic activity must be judged in terms of "Christian tradition", to evaluating it in terms of "commercial common sense, which he is sanguine enough to hope will be Christian".[13] Once the Church chose silence, who was left to speak of economic justice as a matter at least as important as economic growth?

It is important to see the vast gap separating Weber's essay on the role religion played indirectly in the formation of the characteristic personality of the capitalist from Tawney's views on the subject. Rather than one "ethos", Protestantism to Tawney was a house of many mansions, most at war with each other. His focus was on the clash of religious opinion which preceded the abnegation of the social responsibility of the Anglican church, and which in Tawney's own day had been renewed. No relentless march of the ascetic and methodical personality, à la Max Weber, for Tawney. What had been lost could be regained.

It was to this effort that he dedicated his two most important essays in political thought, *The Acquisitive Society* and *Equality*. The first of these works was initially published in the religious periodical the *Hibbert Journal*. His subject was to elucidate the right principles on which the organization of industry should be based. Function and freedom are the terms he gave here to the object of industry and freedom to the control of industry by those whom it serves. A just society, in his view, is one which there is "a community of wills which are often discordant, but which are capable of being inspired by devotion to common ends".[14] This kind of society is not a mechanism, but a fellowship, a recognition of the mutual claims we have on each other in our economic lives. In wartime, the common end was visible; in peacetime it was the business of writers and educators to help people see that the state control of industry was a means to ensure the ends of bringing function and freedom together. And this was all the more important at a time when industrial conflict – which he termed a poison in the *Acquisitive Society* -- was intensifying all over the world. Tawney was not an advocate of class conflict but of finding ethical ways of superseding it. The Christian socialist pointed the way out of strife towards solidarity, perhaps the kind of solidarity he saw among soldiers by his side on the Somme in 1916.

---

[13] *Religion and the rise of capitalism*, p. 116.
[14] *The Acquisitive society*, p. 180.

Equality appeared in 1931, at a time when the economic fortunes of the nation were at their nadir. Unemployment in some towns in northern England had reached 90 per cent of the labour force; 20 percent was the national average. It was in this inclement climate that he made a claim which reiterated his earlier Thomist views on equality but which went beyond them. His premise was that men are not identical, and need no identical treatment by the state or any other institution. They shared common limitations, and these arise from the fact that we all have claims on each other. To this he adds the Kantian proscription against using men as means and not treating them as ends. Only when people recognize the personality of man, a Thomist premise if there ever was one, will they recognize their obligations to each other, and see that those obligations arise from the sameness of people and not from arbitrary distinctions of race, religion, or their material or physical inequality.

Here is the key to Tawney's optimism. "What matters to the health of society is the objective towards which its face is set", and not the distance from achieving it. "A society which is convinced that inequality is an evil", he went on, "need not be alarmed because the evil is one which cannot wholly be subdued. In recognizing the poison it will have armed itself with an antidote. It will have deprived inequality of its sting by stripping it of its esteem".[15] This is the only way to eviscerate the religion of inequality. Only through education – the full development of human personality – and the slow and steady chipping away by teachers and writers like Tawney at the foundations of that unchristian faith will the religion of inequality be exposed as a crime and a delusion and collapse of its own weight. Thus spake Tawney. It is a message not without relevance 80 years after it first appeared in print.

Conclusion

This brief essay has left out much of Tawney's career worth careful study. He was a consistent contributor to the editorial pages of the *Manchester Guardian*, and had a say about educational policy and social policy in general for decades through that newspaper. He was a stalwart of the WEA throughout his life, and a Labour party man through and through. He worked for the League of Nations on a learned study of China's agrarian

---

[15] *Equality*, p. 47.

problems, and served as labour attaché to the British embassy in Washington during the Second World War, producing in the process a history of the American labour movement to guide the ambassador, Lord Halifax, who would not recognize a trade union if he bumped into one.

But it is as an historian and political writer that he made his indelible mark. Tawney was a man of the imperial moment; he turned the *mission civilisatrise* of his childhood in Calcutta into a mission to civilize the English at home. He did so in the same spirit as Gandhi expressed, when he was asked what he thought of Western civilization. His response was that he thought it would be a good idea.

In all his writings, he was more interested in the ethics of wealth distribution than the economics of wealth creation, and hence was a man who never shook off the mantle of the expansive period of British capitalism. If, as Robert Skidelsky put it, socialists needed a robust capitalism to finance its supersession, Tawney was a man whose moral socialism was hard-placed to create a core of policy for the Labour party between the wars. No one, though, tried harder to provide Labour with a set of beliefs not dependent on international economic trends.

Education was Tawney's long-term solution to structural problems, and after his death in 1960, to a degree it has worked in Britain and in parts of Europe. Secondary education is free for all in Britain. The Robbins report of 1962 launched a period of major growth in higher education, and yet the two Englands of Disraeli's time and after survived the democratization of educational provision. The commodification of university education, initiated by Tony Blair's Labour government, and now continued by his successors, was the kind of policy Tawney treated with contempt. It will reinforce educational inequality, and social inequality as a consequence. There is much still in Tawney's writings on education with which to conger today.

His kind of economic history has had a long and round-about fate. Economic history after his death went through a rise through quantification and then a major decline through suspicion and resistance to quantification. His moral concerns resurfaced in the treatment of inequality in the work of the Noble-prize winning economist Amartya Sen, whose ideas were developed in part at the LSE. Sen's emphasis on capabilities and functionings is very close to the model Tawney developed in *Equality*, and Sen's redefinition of the labour theory of value provides echoes of much Tawney wrote on the dignity of manual labour. Here too *la lutte continue*. His kind of economic history informed the labour history of E.P. Thompson and the cultural history of later historians like Gareth Stedman Jones.

Tawney's religious vision of social reform has more of a legacy abroad today than in contemporary Britain, where secularization has taken its toll. Liberation theology, Protestant and Catholic alike, is the home for his belief in equality as the core of the Christian faith. To see the face of Christ, says the Peruvian Dominican Gustavo Gutierrez, we must see the face of the poor, and Tawney might have added, anyone who believes in God has to give that poor man or woman not only respect but the education to live fully and freely the life he or she was given by God.

Among many others, Bishop Trevor Huddleston, of Sharpeville and Stepney, carried Tawney's Christian socialism in the 1960s and 1970s. So did the anti-apartheid movement, the anti-nuclear movement, and a part of the post-1970 human-rights movement. But after the end of the twentieth century, the place of the churches and their teaching in the social and family lives of ordinary people in England is marginal at best. Religious life is not relevant to many younger people, and sociologists have shown clearly that this trend, present in the 1960s, is most evident within the Anglican tradition out of which Tawney came. His religious convictions, I believe, are the key to his vision of politics and education, and those beliefs, so simply stated in his pre-war commonplace book, may very well belong to another world.

Frederick Temple and the *Essays and Reviews* Controversy[1]

Ian Hesketh

---

[1] This chapter was originally presented at the Canadian Society of Church History, Waterloo, Canada, May 2012. I would like to thank Patrick Derham, James Hull, Bernard Lightman, Stuart MacDonald, Geoff Read, and Todd Webb for their helpful comments on the presented version of the paper.

When Frederick Temple was approached in the summer of 1858 to contribute to a volume of essays on religious topics, he was unable to see the storm clouds forming in the distance. That volume, which would be entitled *Essays and Reviews* and in print just two years later, was to follow both the form and style of recently published collections with equally unassuming titles, such as the *Oxford Reviews*, an 1856 volume to which Temple had also previously contributed.[2] Unlike its predecessors, however, *Essays and Reviews* would not be ignored, engendering, in the measured words of Ieuan Ellis, "the greatest religious crisis of the Victorian age."[3]

The crisis lasted from 1860 until 1864, and was briefly revived in 1869, taking "many forms and operat[ing] on many different social levels".[4] The controversy began largely in print thanks to a growing number of reviews that appeared first in the religious weeklies and monthlies later shifting to the national secular quarterlies and newspapers. There were also approximately one hundred and fifty pamphlets directed specifically against *Essays and Reviews*, and most of these appeared by early 1861,[5] as well as several volumes of collected essays.[6] Perhaps most significantly, two of the essayists were charged and tried for heresy by the Church of England thereby adding a legal dimension to the controversy, with the trials and subsequent appeals spawning a whole literature of their own. What is more, side-controversies seemed to appear with every new intervention, to the point where it was difficult to tell where the main controversy stopped and the side-controversies started. Throughout, the essayists were dubbed "Septum contra Christum", the seven against Christ.

And yet it all began rather innocently. Temple was simply asked by one of the other essayists to contribute something on a religious topic that would be in the "liberal direction, but strictly within the limits allowed by the

---

[2] Frederick Temple, "National Education," in *Oxford Essays Contributed by Members of the University* (London, 1856), pp. 218–270.
[3] Ieuan Ellis, *Seven against Christ: A Study of "Essays and Reviews"* (Leiden: E J Brill, 1980), p. ix.
[4] Victor Shea and William Whitla (eds), *Essays and Reviews: The 1860 Text and Its Reading* (Charlottesville and London: University of Virginia Press, 2000), p. 46.
[5] Joseph L. Altholz, *Anatomy of a Controversy: The Debate over "Essays and Reviews"* (Aldershot: Scolar Press, 1994), p. 64.
[6] Shea and Whitla (eds), *Essays and Reviews*, pp. 42–3.

Church of England."⁷ Having agreed to contribute, the piece was never high on Temple's "to do" list. He had only recently begun his tenure as headmaster of Rugby school and had to balance his new duties with previous commitments, always giving priority to the former at the expense the latter. And by all accounts, he was extremely hard working as Rugby's headmaster. Not only was he responsible for a whole host of teaching and administrative duties, he was also the school's chaplain, which required the preaching of daily sermons as well as preparing the boys for confirmation, the arrangements for which were considerably demanding.⁸ And when he was not consumed with his official duties, he was famously climbing the elm trees in the Close, to ensure their sturdiness for the safe climbing of adventurous boys.⁹ Temple, therefore, had little time to work on an essay that was destined to be studied and scrutinized intensely by thousands of readers in the space of just a few years.

H.B. Wilson was in charge of compiling the volume, and therefore was in charge of tracking down any overdue essays, though Temple was by no means the only author behind schedule. Temple eventually responded to Wilson's prodding and submitted a hastily revised sermon that he originally preached at the University of Oxford and also possibly in the Rugby chapel on "The Education of the World"—a brief history of the progressive education of humanity from its primitive to a civilized state that by analogy compared the educational development of the individual from childhood to adult maturity.¹⁰ The essay was effectively a call for the free study of the Bible given that modern English society, according to Temple, was in the manhood stage of development, far beyond the previous stages of youth and childhood, which required stricter rules and discipline to ensure both devotion and continued growth. Now, however, English society was ready for a wider toleration of religious enquiry, one that might challenge previously accepted but, in the end, false dogmas. On its own, the essay would have gone unnoticed as it did when it was a sermon, but as it was the

---

[7] Temple quoted in E.G. Sandford (ed), *Memoirs of Archbishop Temple by Seven Friends*, 2 vols. (London: Macmillan 1906), vol. 2, p. 605; and Peter Hinchliff, *Frederick Temple, Archbishop of Canterbury: A Life* (Oxford: Clarendon Press, 1998), p. 60.
[8] Hinchliff, *Frederick Temple, Archbishop of Canterbury*, pp. 102–103.
[9] Sandford (ed), *Memoirs of Archbishop Temple by Seven Friends*, vol. 1, p. 159; and JB Hope Simpson, *Rugby since Arnold* (London: Macmillan, 1967), p. 42.
[10] Altholz, *Anatomy of a Controversy*, p. 15; Shea and Whitla (eds), *Essays and Reviews*, p. 51

first of seven essays it acted as an introduction setting the stage for what followed in the name of freedom of religious enquiry.

Preceding Temple's essay was a brief prefatory "Note to the Reader" that explained, most notably for the controversy that would follow, that "the Authors of the ensuing Essays are responsible for their respective articles only. They have been written in entire independence of each other, and without concert or comparison."[11] There was indeed little if any coordination between the essayists. Temple claims that he did not know the content of any of the essays until he saw the book in print and that seems to have been the case with the other authors as well. Temple quite literally sent his paper directly to the printer and therefore received no editorial input from Wilson or the other contributors. At least one of the essayists, however, admitted to being somewhat disappointed with Temple's "réchauffé". Wilson had recently heard a different and "far better" sermon preached by Temple at the British Association for the Advancement of Science (BAAS) meeting at Oxford in July of 1860, one that was about "the relations of science to religion" and therefore equally if not more relevant to the line taken in *Essays and Reviews*.[12] Of course, the BAAS meeting of that year is more often noted for the debates generated by Charles Darwin's newly published *Origin of Species*. But just a day after the Bishop of Oxford, Samuel Wilberforce, famously vented his spleen about the encroachment of evolutionary science on religious terrain, Temple's Sunday sermon seemed to suggest quite the opposite, that science and religion were in fact complementary. "The more the Bible is studied," argued Temple, "and the more nature is studied, the deeper will be found the harmony between them in character, the more assured the certainty that whoever inspired the one also made the other."[13] While Wilberforce represents one religiously motivated response to the

---

[11] Altholz, *Anatomy of a Controversy*, p. 15; Shea and Whitla (eds), *Essays and Reviews*, p. 136.

[12] H.B. Wilson to Mark Pattison, 25 July 1860, in Shea and Whitla (eds), *Essays and Reviews*, p. 50

[13] Frederick Temple, *The Present Relations of Science to Religion: A Sermon Preached on Act Sunday, July 1, 1860 before the University of Oxford during the Meeting of the British Association* (Oxford and London: Parker, 1860), p. 17. On Wilberforce at the BAAS in 1860 see Ian Hesketh, *Of Apes and Ancestors: Evolution, Christianity, and the Oxford Debate* (Toronto: University of Toronto Press, 2009).

quickening advance of Victorian science, Temple represents quite another—and one that would become more orthodox as the century progressed.[14]

But in 1860 it would have been impossible to foresee that an unbeliever like Darwin would eventually be buried in Westminster Abbey—and equally so that Temple would eventually become the Archbishop of Canterbury.[15] For now, biblical criticism, evolution, positivism, and uniformitarian geology were fairly new and growing fields of knowledge that posed difficult questions for Anglican believers willing to think about them and consider their implications. Temple was so willing. His strategy was to allow himself the freedom to deliberate without being constrained by Anglican dogma. He believed that by facing these new challenges to the Anglican faith, both truthfully and rationally, Christianity could only be strengthened. As he wrote to his friend, then bishop of London, AC Tait, during the height of the *Essays and Reviews* controversy, he believed that a wide toleration was necessary in considering religious topics even if it may be said that such "will issue in wild and extravagant speculations." He believed that tolerating extreme opinions within the Church would be a "guarantee that the moderate opinions are those held from conviction [and] not from fear of consequences." What is more, he argued, a "wide toleration" would ensure that false extremes that have in the past "lived because they were hunted into the dark" would eventually "die in the light," while clergymen would have "the courage to speak the truth" about continuously perpetuated superstitions such as "the theory of literal interpretation."[16]

Temple's fellow essayists wrote their pieces under the same commitment to the freedom of religious enquiry by considering precisely those contentious subjects that were deemed threatening to the Anglican faith. They were also united in a devotion to new developments in biblical hermeneutics by interpreting the Bible based on its historical and literary

---

[14] See John Hedley Brooke, *Science and Religion: Some Historical Perspectives* (Cambridge: Cambridge University Press, 1991), pp. 274, 310, for a comparison of Temple's and Wilberforce's different responses to Darwin's theory in 1860.

[15] Robert Young also points out the improbability of these two events from the perspective of 1860 in *Darwin's Metaphor: Nature's Place in Victorian Culture* (Cambridge and New York: Cambridge University Press, 1985), p. 149.

[16] Temple to A.C. Tait, 25 February 1861, quoted in Hinchliff, *Frederick Temple, Archbishop of Canterbury*, p. 77.

contexts.[17] Subjects covered by the other six essays included an analysis of recent literature in German biblical criticism (Rowland Williams), the establishment of general principles for the critical study of the Bible (Benjamin Jowett), an analysis of religious tendencies in English history (Mark Pattison), a study of the contemporary relations between church and state (Wilson), an analysis of the vast discrepancies that existed between a literal interpretation of Genesis and recent geological discoveries (CW Goodwin), and a critique of natural theology, particularly the view that miracles somehow provided evidence for the truth of Christianity (Baden Powell).

While none of the essays dealt explicitly with evolution, as Darwin's book was only published as *Essays and Reviews* was in type, the two works were often linked given that they were published in close succession and both seemed to be dedicated to the elevation of evidence-based rationalism at the expense of the authority of and faith in Anglican doctrine. At the time, however, *Essays and Reviews* produced an intense backlash over the space of just a few years that could not be matched by the initially smaller but longer-lasting controversy surrounding Darwin's *Origin of Species*. The sales of the two books are telling in this regard. *On the Origin of Species* sold roughly six thousand copies in its first two years of existence whereas during the same period *Essays and Reviews* sold over twenty thousand, staggering sales for any book, but especially so for a book of theology not named the Bible.[18]

Part of the reason for the explosive nature of the *Essays and Reviews* controversy was the content of the essays certainly, but the furore over the book was perhaps due to the identity of the essayists. They were not lay naturalists tucked away in their country estates but, with the exception of

---

[17] See Shea and Whitla (eds.), *Essays and Reviews*, p. 9 for a description of the developments in nineteenth-century biblical hermeneutics that united the seven essayists.

[18] The total print run of *Essays and Reviews*, from 1860 until 1869, was 24,250 copies. The *Origin* would not reach the 24,000 mark until 1882, the year of Darwin's death. For the print runs of *Essays and Reviews* see Shea and Whitla (eds), *Essays and Reviews*, p. 25; for the print runs of the *Origin* see Bernard Lightman, *Victorian Popularizers of Science: Designing Nature for New Audiences* (Chicago: University of Chicago Press, 2007), p. 34 n. 112. On the printing and selling of the Bible in nineteenth-century Britain see Leslie Howsam, *Cheap Bibles: Nineteenth-Century Publishing and the British and Foreign Bible Society* (Cambridge: Cambridge University Press, 1991).

Goodwin, were reputable clergymen, and in theory devoted to the teachings of the established Church. It was one thing for the Church to be concerned about the threat of rational criticism coming from without, but quite another when it seemed to be coming from within. According to Peter Hinchliff, "it seemed that faith was being stabbed in the back by those who professed to be its friends."[19]

Ironically, the controversy began not with a damning condemnation from a High or Low Church perspective, but rather because of a review that appeared in the radical *Westminster Review*, the one quarterly the essayists assumed would be sympathetic. It was not. The reviewer, a young Frederic Harrison, who had recently joined the ranks of the unbelieving positivists, found the essayists' attempt to preserve a form of "neo-Christianity" in the face of scientific and critical evidence in favour of atheism just plain hypocritical.[20] While the review attacked the book from the far left it had the effect of justifying many of the worst fears of more conservative readers while setting the terms for much of the debate that followed. Most significantly, Harrison challenged the suggestion of the essayists that they were somehow only responsible for their particular essays. It would be "idle to pretend," argued Harrison, "that each writer is not morally responsible for the general tendency of the whole."[21] Temple, in other words, was as responsible for his own essay on the progressive nature of religious understanding as he was for Baden Powell's on the rejection of miracles as evidence for the truth claims of Christianity. As far as Harrison was concerned, the book was not a collection of disconnected essays and reviews but rather a party manifesto announcing a new and essentially suicidal form of rationalized Christianity. The review was apparently distributed during the BAAS meeting that year, most notably amongst a large group of Oxford clergyman who had gathered following the Wilberforce–Huxley debate, and it indeed "excite[d] their horror."[22]

If Harrison's review had the effect of alerting many to the existence of the half-heartedly heretical volume, Samuel Wilberforce sought to rally the

---

[19] Hinchliff, *Frederick Temple, Archbishop of Canterbury*, p. 68.
[20] Frederic Harrison, "Neo-Christianity," *Westminster Review* 146 (Oct, 1860): 293–332, at 322.
[21] *Ibid* at 294.
[22] Evelyn Abbott and Lewis Campbell, *The Life and Letters of Benjamin Jowett*, vol. 1, 3rd edn (New York: P. Button and Co, 1897), p. 292.

members of the Church against it in his lengthy condemnation that appeared in the *Quarterly Review* early in 1861. His strategy was one of divide and conquer. Not only did Wilberforce repeat Harrison's argument about the joint responsibility of the authors, he took the argument one step further, declaring that "every writer in [the book] who does not, by some after act, visibly separate himself from the fellowship of opinions to which he is here committed" must be condemned along with the book as a whole.[23] Wilberforce would later explicitly single out Temple, whose essay, Wilberforce admitted, did not present the outward signs of atheism made so clear by some of the other essayists but that he should be condemned just the same. Unless, of course, "Dr. Temple has himself been shocked to find what the edifice is to which he has been led unconsciously to furnish the portal. If this be so, as we trust it is, the least atonement he can make to the Church, upon the members of which he has brought suspicion, is that he should, with the manly openness which we believe marks his character, disclaim his agreement with the views with which he is here connected."[24] He also knew that Temple was seemingly vulnerable in his current position. He had only been headmaster at Rugby for three years. And Wilberforce cleverly pointed out that Temple was in charge of some of the nation's most promising youth, suggesting that "we should tremble, not only for the faith, but for the morals of his pupils."[25] Clearly Soapy Sam, as Wilberforce was often called for his slipperiness in ecclesiastical debates, was not afraid to get a little dirty – and thereby add another dimension to his nickname – if it meant dividing the essayists amongst themselves.

At the same time as Wilberforce was calling attention to Temple's position as an educator of the nation's youth, Temple's more conservative friends were trying to make it easy for him to do just what Wilberforce wanted and separate himself from the other essayists. Tait, who was one of Temple's predecessors at Rugby and was also instrumental in securing Temple's appointment, did what he could behind the scenes as bishop of London to keep Temple from being grouped together with the other essayists. Tait suggested to his fellow bishops that Temple should be explicitly excluded from any general condemnation of the book but such an exception could only be made if Temple was willing to make some sort of

---

[23] [Samuel Wilberforce], "Essays and Reviews," *Quarterly Review* 109 (Jan, 1861): 248–306, at 251.
[24] *Ibid* at 251–2.
[25] *Ibid* at 256.

statement distancing himself from the other essayists. Tait even suggested perhaps publishing a selection of their correspondence, which would make clear Temple's differences with the other essayists without being the explicitly public declaration that Wilberforce favoured. In the end, Temple refused to separate himself from the essayists in any form and was angered that Tait seemed to be lining up with the other bishops in condemning the volume.[26]

While Temple was willing to endanger long friendships over his connection with the book, he was more sympathetic to the concerns of Rugby parents and the trustees who were beginning to make noise about the radical headmaster and the supposedly heretical ideas being spread throughout the school. And certainly the trustees and parents had cause for concern. The headmaster was greatly admired by the boys who were clearly taken with Temple's very personal style of education which encouraged the "cultivation" (a favourite word of Temple's) of moral qualities and mental discipline rather than rote learning. According to Temple, the teacher should not just be a medium of knowledge for the students but more importantly should act as a role model.[27] The boys at Rugby responded to Temple's educational ideals only too well. As one boy wrote to his mother during the height of the *Essays and Reviews* controversy, "Temple's all right, but if he turns Mahommedan, the whole School will turn Mahommedan too."[28] It was comments such as this that helped to justify Wilberforce's trembling for Temple's pupils.

Needless to say, Temple was also concerned about what the boys thought about his association with a supposedly heretical collection of essays. He decided to meet with them and the masters in order to explain that perhaps it was a blunder to let his essay be published in the volume after he had already taken up his position at Rugby. With that said, however, he still believed that the book itself "ought to have been published. The book

---

[26] For the rift between Temple and Tait see Hinchliff, *Frederick Temple, Archbishop of Canterbury*, pp. 70–82.
[27] *Ibid* pp. 43–44. For Temple's views on education see Temple, "National Education"; and Simon Green, "Archbishop Frederick Temple on Meritocracy," in Michael Bentley (ed.), *Public and Private Doctrine: Essays in British History Presented to Maurice Cowling* (Cambridge: Cambridge University Press, 1993), pp. 149–167.
[28] Simpson, *Rugby since Arnold*, p. 44; and see Hinchliff, *Frederick Temple, Archbishop of Canterbury*, p. 58.

contains opinions which had long been lurking in corners; it was time they were dragged to light and faced." He explained that the essayists all agreed that they were only responsible for their particular essays and therefore should not be held accountable for the views of others. But he warned the boys "against entering on the speculations contained in that book in a light and cursory way, and against supposing that I agree with all that is in that book. I am sure that you know me too well to suppose this for an instant."[29] Apparently Temple was not quite ready to lead a mass conversion to Islam.

The trustees held a meeting of their own, in April 1861, to discuss the controversy and question Temple, who proved to be an evasive interviewee as he refused to discuss anything other than the running of the school. On this front, it would have been difficult to find much fault with Temple. At this point only five boys had been removed from the school as a result of the controversy; moreover, the school itself was fully booked until 1866. There was little doubt that Temple's headmastership marked a significant turnaround for the school, which suffered from declining enrolment during the tenure of Temple's predecessor, EM Goulburn. Given the relatively positive outlook for the school as well as Temple's rather sincere meeting with the boys and masters, his position as headmaster of Rugby school was seemingly never in doubt.[30]

As the bishops were content to let the Rugby trustees deal with Temple, it seemed that for the time being, he had weathered the storm. Wilson and Rowland Williams were not so lucky. The two were tried for heresy in the ecclesiastical courts and a few passages in their essays were found contrary to specific Thirty-nine Articles, the articles of Anglican faith that both Wilson and Williams would have sworn oaths to on entering Holy Orders. They were therefore found guilty and suspended from their positions for a year. However, much to the irritation of the bishops, the sentences were overturned in the secular appeals court as the passages in question were ambiguous enough to leave doubt in the new judge's mind about their intended meaning. In response, the bishops decided to vote on a blanket

---

[29] Sandford (ed.), *Memoirs of Archbishop Temple by Seven Friends*, vol. 1, p. 220 n.; and Hinchliff, *Frederick Temple, Archbishop of Canterbury*, p. 76.
[30] Simpson, *Rugby since Arnold*, pp. 53–6; and Hinchliff, *Frederick Temple, Archbishop of Canterbury*, pp. 54, 87. Note that Simpson claims three boys were withdrawn whereas Hinchliff claims that there were five. On the declining numbers during Goulburn's headmastership see Simpson, *Rugby since Arnold*, p. 24.

condemnation of the book at Convocation, which included almost twelve thousand clergymen. The condemnation passed. So instead of two authors being found guilty of heresy, the book itself was synodically condemned "as containing teaching contrary to the doctrine received by the United Church of England and Ireland, in common with the whole Catholic Church of Christ."[31]

There things stood until the controversy was briefly re-born when Prime Minister Gladstone suggested Temple's name as a candidate for the vacant see of Exeter in 1869. Many clergymen were outraged that an essayist in a book officially condemned by the Church of England could even be considered for a bishopric. It did not help matters that Charles Longman, the publisher of *Essays and Reviews*, published the last edition of the book with a single change describing Temple as "Bishop elect of Exeter".[32] Wilberforce, once again, led the charge to mobilize the clergy against Temple's candidacy and once again Temple refused publically to separate himself from the other essayists. It was only after he was confirmed that he admitted that he should remove his name from future printings of the book. As he stated on February 11 to the Upper House of Convocation, "I felt certainly that the publication of one essay amongst others was a thing which might be allowed to Frederick Temple, but which was not, therefore, to be allowed to the Bishop of Exeter". He was concerned that his new position would give the book "a kind of authority it would not have of itself".[33] Many of his liberal friends felt somewhat betrayed, but it is significant that Temple waited until after the consecration to remove his name rather than before when it would have been more politically expedient. What is more, during the height of the controversy, Temple consented to Longman's reprinting of the last edition, given the renewed interest in the volume, while requesting that this would be the final printing.[34]

It has often been argued that Temple became more conservative in his religious beliefs as he aged, in part because he moved up the Anglican

---

[31] For the full text of the synodical condemnation see Shea and Whitla (eds), *Essays and Reviews*, pp. 672–676; see also Altholz, *Anatomy of a Controversy*, pp. 123–4.
[32] *Ibid* p. 136; cf. Shea and Whitla (eds), *Essays and Reviews*, p. 128 n. 9.
[33] The full text of "Temple's Address to the Upper House of Convocation" can be found in Shea and Whitla (eds), *Essays and Reviews*, p. 684–686; see also Altholz, *Anatomy of a Controversy*, p. 139.
[34] Shea and Whitla (eds), *Essays and Reviews*, p. 21.

hierarchy, and seemingly did so at the expense of his past allegiances, both personal and professional.[35] But this overly simplifies things. While he may have shifted towards the High Church when it came to issues of upholding the authority of the Church of England, he was central in helping to liberalize the Church's position concerning science, particularly that of evolution.[36] Indeed, if Wilberforce's views about science and religion were the seemingly orthodox position of the Anglican Church in the 1860s, by the 1880s it is safe to say that Temple's were in the ascendant. In 1884 Temple was invited to give the Bampton lectures and he did so on "the relations between science and religion" thereby returning to a subject he had preached on at the 1860 BAAS meeting. Much had changed in the intervening twenty-four years. Not only was the supposed "German rationalism" that had so angered High and Low Churchman becoming the accepted standard for "conventions of literary, historical, and biblical studies,"[37] evolution was no longer the terrifying threat to man's place in nature as God's special creation. Forms of Christian evolution had become much more widespread as space was either found or made in Darwin's system for purpose and progressive direction. Temple, for his part, argued that evolution could not present a more wonderful illustration of God's omnipotence. As Temple so eloquently argued, under evolutionary theory God "did not make the things, we must say; no, but He made them make themselves."[38] It was for this reason that Temple argued that "Science, in teaching Evolution, has yet asserted anything that is inconsistent with Revelation".[39] These views gained even more legitimacy within the Church after Temple became Archbishop of

---

[35] Hinchliff examines some of Temple's seemingly High Church views in *Frederick Temple, Archbishop of Canterbury*, pp. 236, 239–240, 256–257.

[36] As Owen Chadwick argues, the election of Temple as Archbishop of Canterbury "may be taken to mark the final acceptance of the doctrine of evolution among the divines, clergy and leading laity of the established church, at least as a doctrine permissible and respectable in an eminent clergyman. For no one who disbelieved evolution, and thought it incompatible with the faith of a Christian bishop, lodged a protest." Chadwick, *The Victorian Church*, 2 vols. (London: Adam & Charles Black, 1970), vol. 2, p. 23.

[37] Shea and Whitla (eds), *Essays and Reviews*, p. 7.

[38] Frederick Temple, *The Relations between Religion and Science: Eight Lectures Preached before the University of Oxford in the Year 1884* (New York: Macmillan, 1884), p. 115. For an analysis of Temple's evolutionary views and the relationship between science and religion see Hinchliff, *Frederick Temple, Archbishop of Canterbury*, ch. 7.

[39] Temple, *The Relations between Religion and Science*, p. 188.

Canterbury in 1896. Unlike his election as bishop of Exeter, this time there was no re-enacting of the *Essays and Reviews* controversy.

References

Altholz, J.L. (1994) *Anatomy of a Controversy: The Debate over "Essays and Reviews."* Aldershot: Scolar Press.

Brooke, J.H. (1991) *Science and Religion: Some Historical Perspectives*. Cambridge: Cambridge University Press.

Chadwick, O. (1970) *The Victorian Church*, 2 vols. London: Adam & Charles Black.

Ellis, I. (1980) *Seven against Christ: A Study of "Essays and Reviews."* Leiden: E J Brill.

Green, S. (1993) "Archbishop Frederick Temple on Meritocracy," in M Bentley (ed.), *Public and Private Doctrine: Essays in British History Presented to Maurice Cowling*. Cambridge: Cambridge University Press.

Harrison, F. (1860) "Neo-Christianity," *Westminster Review* 146 (Oct.): 293–332.

Hesketh, I. (2009) *Of Apes and Ancestors: Evolution, Christianity, and the Oxford Debate*. Toronto: University of Toronto Press.

Hinchliff, P. (1998) *Frederick Temple, Archbishop of Canterbury: A Life*. Oxford: Clarendon Press.

Howsam, L. (1991) *Cheap Bibles: Nineteenth-Century Publishing and the British and Foreign Bible Society*. Cambridge: Cambridge University Press.

Lightman, B. (2007) *Victorian Popularizers of Science: Designing Nature for New Audiences*. Chicago: University of Chicago Press.

Sandford, E.G. (ed). (1906) *Memoirs of Archbishop Temple by Seven Friends*, 2 vols. London: Macmillan.

Shea, V and Whitla, W (eds). (2000) *Essays and Reviews: The 1860 Text and Its Reading*. Charlottesville and London: University of Virginia Press, 2000.

Simpson, J.B.H. (1967) *Rugby since Arnold*. London: Macmillan.

Temple, F. (1856) "National Education," in *Oxford Essays Contributed by Members of the University*. London.

Temple, F. (1860) *The Present Relations of Science to Religion: A Sermon Preached on Act Sunday, July 1, 1860 before the University of Oxford during the Meeting of the British Association*. Oxford and London: Parker.

Temple, F. (1884) *The Relations between Religion and Science: Eight Lectures Preached before the University of Oxford in the Year 1884*. New York: Macmillan.

Young, R. (1985) *Darwin's Metaphor: Nature's Place in Victorian Culture*. Cambridge and New York: Cambridge University Press.

R. G. Collingwood: The Totality of Experience

David Boucher

For his whole life, beginning in 1889, Robin George Collingwood felt he was swimming against the tide. At his death on 9 January, 1943 Collingwood was one of the last adherents to a philosophy that had gradually fallen from favour since the end of the First World War. He never fully embraced philosophical Idealism in its entirety and felt that in many respects, in logic, metaphysics and aesthetics, he had made advances on it. Nevertheless, the pre-eminent place of thought and ideas in shaping reality always remained an important feature of his philosophy. Confident by nature, he was forthright in his opinions on almost every issue. His writings are combative, taking a stand against prevailing interpretations in history, or developing an original argument in philosophy by confronting hallowed orthodoxies, and challenging received wisdom on the Roman occupation of Britain. His interests were catholic, ranging from philosophy, literature, scientific thought, music, anthropology, archaeology and sailing. As an archaeologist he was renowned throughout the world as the foremost expert on the Roman inscriptions in Britain. He inherited from his mentor Francis Haverfield, at Oxford, the mantle of ensuring what was a relatively unfashionable period in Roman History, the later Roman occupation, did not sink without trace. He discharged his obligation to Haverfield with remarkable success. As well as detailed archaeological work, he was an extremely talented synthesiser of the extraordinary number of amateur and professional reports from digs throughout the country (Collingwood, 1932; Collingwood, [1936] 1937). With his father he co-edited the *Transactions of the Cumberland and Westmorland Antiquarian and Archaeological Society* (1921-25) and continued to do so with others until 1935, when he became the Waynflete Professor of Metaphysical Philosophy at Magdalen College, Oxford. His accomplishments in drawing and collecting the Roman Inscriptions in Britain were not fully appreciated until 1965 with their posthumous publication (Collingwood and Wright, [1965] 1995). His father was an archaeologist as well as talented painter and author, best known for his two volume biography of Ruskin, for whom he acted as secretary (W. G. Collingwood, 1893). W. G. Collingwood provided the exemplar for his son. A painter; translator and writer of Norse sagas; designer of Celtic crosses and war memorials; archaeologist and adventurer, he and his wife Edith (known as Dorrie or Molly) taught Robin and his sisters at home. Formal lessons took place in a few hours set aside each morning. These included Greek, Latin, and ancient and modern history. Collingwood was left to his own devices for the rest of the day to pursue, on his own, with friends or family, anything that fired his imagination. It was during these early years that Collingwood developed his passion for philosophy and natural science (Collingwood, 1939: 7-8). He read Kant's Theory of Ethics at the age of eight and was disappointed in himself for not understanding it. He also interested himself in natural scientific theories and concluded that science was less a cumulative body of truths and more like an organism continuously changing. This later found expression in *An Essay on Metaphysics* (1940) and *The Idea of Nature* (1945).

Whereas his own account of his childhood paints a picture of a precocious child, the evidence of his juvenilia betrays a more frivolous, and vulnerable side. A boy interested in Rudyard Kipling's *Captain Courageous* as well as Baden Powell and the Scouting movement, excited that his father was going to buy him a uniform, and had taught him to measure heights. He tells us: 'I have already learnt from BP how to measure the width of rivers, and practised it a little' (Collingwood, April 19th, 1900; and April 3rd, 1900). With his three sisters he also produced various family magazines which included news, short serial stories of fiction, illustrations and maps, written or drawn by the children themselves. The whole family busied itself in prodigious letter writing; story-telling; musical composition; sketching and painting, as well as more formal academic work.

It was not until he was thirteen that Robin entered formal education at Mr Podmore's boarding school, Charney Hall, Grange-over-Sands, from which he won one of ten scholarships to Rugby in 1903, for £60, coming sixth in the nationwide competition. It was the year in which Scarlet Fever ravaged Rugby School, and scholarship examinations had to take place outside. At Charney Hall Collingwood adjusted well to formal school life, and became passionate about soccer, although not very good. This allegiance changed to rugby football, at which he was much better, when he entered Rugby School. Unfortunately, a serious injury to the knee, sustained by an over-vigorous tackle permanently damaged his knee. The masters who impressed and inspired him most were Charles Paget 'Tiger' Hastings, teaching History, and Robert Whitelaw, form master to the Twenty, comprising the most gifted sixth formers. Although the injury to the knee curtailed his sporting career, he threw himself with enthusiasm into the life of the School. He spoke on patriotism in his first debating society speech, and later unsuccessfully defended socialism. The very term 'socialism' illicited fear and loathing among the boys, and Collingwood delighted in bating them with its positive side as the exemplar of justice, truth, love and morality. He was popular among his friends and schoolmasters, becoming head of Wilson's house for two years from 1906. He often returned to Rugby while an undergraduate at University College, Oxford, and Fellow of Pembroke College, to visit old friends and give occasional talks. In December, 1909 for example, he gave a talk on Ewe Close, a prehistoric village settlement near Crosby Ravensworth village, believed to have been occupied by the Romans, and excavated by his father with him as assistant (W.G. Collingwood, 1907-8 and TS Private Collection: FLTR02720).[1] His letters betray a fondness for his schooldays and the many friendships he made which were formative in his life, among them Arthur Cockin, later vicar of St Mary's Oxford where Collingwood delivered lay sermons; Ernest Altounyan, his future brother-in-law; and Angus Graham, whose sister Ethel became his first wife. His letters home during his Rugby years include fascinating portraits of daily life, and pen and pencil sketches of the buildings, interiors and masters. The day began at Rugby at 6-15am, a cold bath at 6-30, followed by weak coffee and biscuits; chapel at 7-00 and the first lesson at 7-15; all before breakfast at 8-15. The letters also reveal the darker side of school life when discipline was kept with the use of the birch and knotted cane. The birch was not used excessively, perhaps twice a term for serious offences, such as swearing. These were the days when neatness of handwriting and tidiness of mind were highly valued. Mrs Podmore, the Headmaster's wife of Charney Hall, for example, thought his neatness would take him far (Letter from Edith Collingwood to her husband, July 28, 1903, signed Molly. Collingwood Society), and the Rev Dr James, Headmaster of Rugby, in his report for Trinity Term 1908, remarked: 'A boy of great culture and refinement both of mind and character. I am sorry to lose him, but I am sure he goes from here to a University career...'

Despite sending his own children to public school, Collingwood came to resent the type of formal education provided, believing it to be stultifying and suffocating, expressing these sentiments in *An Autobiography* (1939), and *The New Leviathan* (1942) in which he put forward his alternative, giving a central role to parents, and in which teachers should be on tap and not on top. The insidious undermining of parental authority in education, he argued, began in Ancient Greece: 'Plato is the man who planted on the European world the crazy idea that education ought to be professionalised; and, as if that were not enough, the crazier idea that the profession ought to be a public service' (Collingwood, 1940: 311).

---

[1] I would like to thank Teresa Smith, Collingwood's daughter, for allowing me to use material from her private archive for this chapter, and for her help and encouragement over the years.

In 1908 he entered University College, Oxford, where his father had studied and been tutored by Bernard Bosanquet. It was at this time that Collingwood became an insomniac precipitating his long-term ill-health. In 1910 he took a first in Classical Moderations and in 1912 a first in *Literae Humaniores*. He was then elected to a philosophy fellowship at Pembroke College. During the First World War Collingwood did unpaid service in Admiralty Intelligence, where he recruited his father and sister Barbara, and joined the philosopher Samuel Alexander. In 1927 he became University Lecturer in Philosophy and Roman History. Collingwood was elected a Fellow of the British Academy in 1934 and in 1935 he was appointed Waynflete Professor of Metaphysical Philosophy, which he resigned on grounds of ill health in 1941. In 1942 he returned to his late father's home, Lanehead in Coniston, with Kathleen Edwardes his second wife.

Collingwood died of pneumonia on 9 January, 1943 at Lanehead a few weeks before his fifty-fourth birthday. The series of strokes he suffered during the late nineteen thirties ensured his early demise. On 12 January, in heavy rain with the mountains enveloped in a black rolling mist, Collingwood was buried by Canon Wilcox and the Reverend R. B. Luard Selby, Collingwood's brother-in-law, the husband of his younger sister Ursula. He is buried in the churchyard in Coniston, marked by an unassuming stone between his parents and John Ruskin.

Achievements

While famous and influential as an archaeologist R. G. Collingwood's enduring reputation is in the area of philosophy, particularly in the philosophy of history and aesthetics (Collingwood, 1938; Collingwood, [1946] 1995; Collingwood, 1999), but he has also made a considerable impact in the field of Metaphysics. Among the luminaries of modern philosophy who have paid homage to him are the Americans John Rawls and Rex Martin; the Australian, Alan Donagan; the Canadians Charles Taylor, W. H. Dray and Lionel Rubinoff; and the British A. J. Ayer, Alistair Macintyre, Bernard Williams, Stephen Toulmin and Quentin Skinner. Among the continental Europeans Collingwood influenced and impressed are Hans Georg Gadamer, Paul Ricoeur, and Agnes Heller. His books, especially in the philosophy of history and aesthetics, are still central to the study of those disciplines.

His crowning achievement in an age of positivism was to establish the differentiae and intellectual integrity of history as a form of knowledge, giving it a centrality to the human sciences and stemming the tide of logical positivism, whose leading British exponent came to concede Collingwood's importance for twentieth century philosophy (Ayer, 1977: 79: Ayer, 1984: 191-213).

The key to understanding the work of Collingwood and the considerable influence he has had on a wide range of disciplines, including statistics, psychology, library classification, aesthetics and history, is that he does not view philosophy as a disinterested activity as, for example, Ludwig Wittgenstein, A. J. Ayer, T. D. Weldon and Michael Oakeshott did. All thought, in his view, was for the sake of action (Boucher, 1995). Every excursion into philosophical analysis was for the purpose of self-knowledge of the mind. History, for example, is not merely about the past, but reveals to us the immense achievements of human thought, and opens up for us the possibilities and full potential of the mind. Art is not merely about aesthetic sensibility, but of crucial importance to civilisation in that it is the expression of spontaneous emotion, which if suppressed results in the corruption of consciousness and a distorted awareness of ourselves and our society. In *An Autobiography* Collingwood maintains that the philosophies to which we subscribe have practical implications for the way we act. To be a utilitarian, for example, is to view the world instrumentally, and consequentially, in terms of means and ends. It was, in his view, a partial view of action, incomplete in that all purposive activity may be understood in terms of utility, that is, as a means to an end; right, or rule governed; and duty, that is, given the sort of person one is, it was the only thing he or she could have done.

Assessing Collingwood's achievements is complicated by the fact that during his life-time some of his most important work remained unpublished. T. M. Knox, a former student of Collingwood's, made the first editorial judgment which proved to be rather severe and narrowly focused. He disregarded Collingwood's own judgment on *The Principles of History*, taking only one chapter from it and including it with previously published and unpublished lectures to produce Collingwood's most famous, but not altogether representative, work of philosophy (Collingwood, [1947] 1993). It is from this book that quotations from Collingwood, a master of overstatement, are most often reproduced out of context and examined in a manner wholly inconsistent with the principles of interpretation that the book itself is propounding. Such statements as, for example, 'All history is the history of thought', or 'history is the re-enactment of past thought', premised on the view that we can re-enact thoughts but not emotions. It was not until 1999 and 2005 when *The Principles of History* and Folk Tales Manuscripts were respectively published, that we see the significance of Knox's initial judgments and exclusions. In these books, the importance of emotions in anthropological and historical studies is affirmed by elaborating upon ideas articulated in *The Principles of Art*.

Idealism and Realism

Collingwood disliked being associated with the idealist movement in philosophy – it was after all an unpopular and disparaged philosophy -- and underplayed it considerably in his *An Autobiography*, but privately, for example, in his letters to the Italians Guido de Ruggiero and Benedetto Croce, he readily confessed to being a Hegelian. He took issue with the philosophical realism of G. E. Moore, Bertrand Russell, John Cook Wilson and the early Ludwig Wittgenstein. He took the main thrust of Realism to be the proposition that knowing makes no difference to the thing that is known. In his view the contention was logically flawed because it entailed knowledge of the object, both before and after knowing it, which is impossible. A more serious error was its avoidance of almost any positive doctrines by relentlessly disintegrating them by criticism. For example, in moral philosophy they rejected over two thousand years of taking its purpose to be thinking more clearly about the issues of personal conduct in order to improve the way one acts. Students exposed to realism were told that philosophical thinking is a disinterested activity with no contribution to make to practical conduct. Bertrand Russell denied that ethics is a proper subject matter for philosophy, while H. H. Prichard thought moral philosophy was purely theoretical, whose task was to focus upon the workings of the moral consciousness, with no reference to its practice. Collingwood rejected such views pointing out that, in contrast, the previous generation of students brought up on the Idealism of T. H. Green, another former pupil of Rugby School, had been taught that clear philosophical thinking is essential to informing and improving conduct. The separation of theory and practice, Collingwood objected, is insidious, not least because it denied the role of the committed intellectual, and absolved the philosopher of social responsibility.

As far as Collingwood was concerned Realists violated all his golden rules; they failed to satisfy themselves by reading texts historically as to the relevance of their criticisms, nor did they take the trouble to determine the question authors asked themselves. Instead they assumed that the questions were perennial. Their most serious crime was to ignore the claims of history as a legitimate form of knowledge, formulating their own theory of knowledge on the methodology of the natural sciences.

Collingwood was, nevertheless, impressed by A.J. Ayer's formulation of the principles of logical positivism, which recognised only synthetic or analytical and empirical or inductive knowledge, the former true by definition and the latter based on observation. Collingwood's *An Essay on Metaphysics* was an ingenious attempt to rescue metaphysics from Ayer's argument that metaphysical statements were neither analytical nor inductive and therefore incapable of conforming to the principle of verification, they were, for Ayer, nonsense statements. Collingwood argued that metaphysical statements were more than presuppositions, but in fact absolute presuppositions, that is, they were ideas upon which the rest of our knowledge was built: they are the foundations upon which thought rests. An example would be belief in God, upon which our whole world view may be predicated, but of whose existence we could not provide proof. Another would be the idea that everything has a cause, which is absolutely presupposed by Newtonian Mechanics, but not by Einstein's physics. Metaphysical statements are absolute presuppositions and not propositions.

Collingwood argued that Ayer was wrong in thinking that the verification principle had to be applied to metaphysical statements. Instead, the work of the metaphysician is to uncover what absolute presuppositions were being absolutely presupposed at any given time. That is why he calls it an historical science, much to the chagrin of many philosophers. Ayer was right in describing metaphysical statements as devoid of the features of propositions, but completely misunderstood what sort of statements they were. Propositions are answers to questions and are either true of false, whereas metaphysical statements are not answers to questions, but instead give rise to questions, and are either absolutely presupposed or they are not. We do not derive Absolute Presuppositions from experience.

Aesthetics

In the field of aesthetics Collingwood's name is synonymous with the theory which claims that art is the expression of emotion. More than anyone else he tried to understand why we should care whether something is a work of art or not. Unlike Wittgenstein, for example, he offers us a criterion for judging success and failure in art. In *Speculum Mentis* he had followed Croce in identifying the distinguishing feature of art to be pure imagination, with its practical side manifest in play. In *Outlines of a Philosophy of Art* (1925) he explores this idea much more thoroughly using the analogy of a spiral staircase to characterise the relation in which each of the different forms, or manners, of experience – art, religion, science, history, philosophy -- stand in relation to each other. His aim is not merely to follow the likes of others such Coleridge and Croce who subscribe to the same idea, but also to draw-out the full implications of conceiving art as pure imagination. The life of the imagination is something in which all human beings participate as a phase of consciousness that is always transcended. The work of art the artist creates, in advancing his or her own artistic life, is in principle capable of advancing that of others. In the act of creating a work of art the artist is trying to see something for himself or herself, and in exhibiting it trying to show others the same thing (Collingwood, [1924] 1994: 88-101).

Collingwood significantly revised his ideas on aesthetics in his 1937 book *The Principles of Art* in which art still involves imagination, of course, but the emphasis is more on the expression of emotion. The audience is elevated to the status of fellow artist: 'the reader is an artist as well as the writer. . . . The poet is . . . singular in his ability to take the initiative in expressing what all feel, and all can express' (Collingwood, 1937: 118-9). As the expression of emotion art differs from craft and magic because both exhibit a utilitarian means/end relationship. The object in craft is conceived for its practical purpose, and then made to fulfil that purpose. For example, an ornate drinking vessel used for communion in church. Its features may be aesthetically pleasing, but the vessel is not art because it is not the spontaneous expression of emotion, but instead a preconceived design for a specific practical purpose. In magic emotions are deliberately evoked, by for example ritual or dance, in order to arouse specific emotions and suppress others. In a war dance fearlessness and courageousness eclipse cowardice, in order to achieve a specific practical outcome. Art as amusement, Collingwood suggests, is nothing more than pseudo art because it deliberately arouses emotions that are immediately dissipated. The arousal of the emotion becomes a substitute for action. Pornography, for instance, is a substitute for sex, whereas the arousal of emotion in magic, such as a fertility ritual is the preparation for sex. Art, understood properly, is not premeditated, it is the formation of an emotion that is acknowledged in its expression. He is using the term expression in a special sense here which distinguishes between betraying an emotion, when one blushes from embarrassment, for example, and expression proper when one first feels something but does not know what it is until it is expressed. The work of art and the expression of emotion cannot be separated. The emotion is not first formulated and then expressed (Collingwood, 1937: 26). This is in fact a rebuttal of Tolstoy's theory of art. In answer to the question 'what is it I feel?', the answer is in the expression (Ridley, 1998: 32). The identification of art with the expressions of emotion, and suppressing emotion with the corruption of a healthy consciousness, permitted Collingwood to conclude that when a person expresses his or her feelings sufficiently to make them accessible to others, he or she has produced a work of art. The artist, then, is engaged in self-exploration and the enhanced self-understanding attained is manifest in the work of art itself. One of the major criticisms of the expression theory, which John Dewey tried to avoid by giving emphasis to the artist's struggle with materials, is that it gives too much weight in the aesthetic judgment to the artist and the agonies of creation, rather than to the object itself, which appears peripheral to the aesthetic consciousness. Collingwood was not, however, concerned with the criteria of 'good' works of art, but instead with the relation between art and mental activity. Art, for him is not a separate activity, but one which permeates all other forms of experience.

Political Philosophy

Throughout his life Collingwood interested himself in political issues and addressed them in his writings, culminating in *The New Leviathan*. It was an aspect of his thought that remained relatively neglected until the late 1980s, largely due to the preface of the *Idea of History* in which the editor Malcolm Knox dismissed Collingwood's later work as the ravings of a dying man. The original sub-title of the *New Leviathan* was *The Principles of Politics* and complemented *The Principles of History* (which remained incomplete). History is self-knowledge of the mind, and the *New Leviathan* gives an account of the development of the European mind. In *New Leviathan* history is the highest form of theoretical reason. The *New Leviathan* is concerned with the levels of practical reason, utility, right and duty, and their relation to society and civilization. Duty, the highest level of practical reason, is the counterpart of history.

His final book is consistent with Idealism with its emphasis on the development and unfolding of freedom, which is the essence of the mind. Freedom develops by reason gradually eliminating caprice from rational choices. Free rational choice, or self-determination, may be impeded by force, physical or psychological, and the aim of the ruling class in the body politic is as far as practicable to eliminate force. Collingwood's political philosophy is a self-conscious, if unorthodox, contribution to the social contract tradition, long before John Rawls revived it and made it fashionable. Collingwood attempts to provide the social contract with an historical dimension. He aims to demonstrate that for each society a process of conversion is taking place from the non-social to the social community, and depending upon the complexity of the society the level of cognitive competence required to satisfy the criteria for conversion vary historically, and geographically. The ruling class is constantly being replenished in this conversion process. His criticism of the social contract tradition exemplified by Hobbes, Locke and Rousseau, is that it fails to supply us with a theory of this on-going historical process of conversion in the body politic. Because of the historical element in his philosophy Collingwood is often accused of being a relativist. This is certainly not the case in *The New Leviathan*. Reason defined as the gradual elimination of caprice; freedom as the capacity for rational choice; and civility as the gradual elimination of force, constitute universal criteria by which to judge civilizations and the degree to which barbarism, that is, the conscious subversion of these ideals, is present in them.

Philosophy of History

Collingwood's most notable contribution to philosophy has been in the area of the philosophy of history. Collingwood is the reference point against which all serious discussions of the subject are measured. The transformation that occurred in the study of political thought during the 1960s, for example, and which reverberates in the present is directly attributable to him, in that its leading proponents, J. G. A. Pocock, John Dunn and above all Quentin Skinner, all acknowledged Collingwood's profound influence. The posthumously published *Idea of History* first determines and evaluates the development of historical principles from Thucydides to the present, identifying the conditions for attaining historical knowledge. All bodies of knowledge which have embedded in them criteria of success and failure, what Collingwood calls criteriological, are scientific. History is based on rational principles and inferred from evidence. Collingwood argues that there is no meaning in history apart from that to be discerned in the activities of people in their relations with each other.

For Collingwood the past is a living past, and in order to know it the historian has to rethink, or re-enact it. Re-enactment is central to his whole philosophy, and those who dismiss it, while extrapolating other aspects of his thought, underestimate its importance. The doctrine enables Collingwood to overcome some of the central dualisms in philosophy, such as the mind/object dichotomy; the idea that the past is not alive at all, but a dead past; and the unification of the inside and the outside of an event.

Collingwood's *The Principles of History* was never completed, but parts IV and V of *The Idea of History* and much of *An Autobiography* provide discussions of what Collingwood intended to cover. In *An Autobiography* we have the logic of question and answer. The meaning of each statement can only be fully understood in relation to the question to which it gave rise. Each statement is an answer to a question, and in turn each question is itself an answer relative to another prior question. It followed for Collingwood that no two propositions are contradictory unless they were meant as answers to the same question. The logic of question and answer was central to one of Collingwood's most contentious claims, that there are no perennial problems in philosophy -- the most sacred of cows among philosophers whose encounters with past thinkers are often ahistorical. We cannot say, for example, that Thomas Hobbes in the seventeenth century is addressing the same question as Plato in Ancient Greece when they discuss the purpose of the state. The terms of reference relate to their own question and answer complexes. That is not to say that the two understandings are unrelated. They are both part of the same historical process by which one conception of the state turns into the other, and the historian may fruitfully contribute to our understanding of it.

Critics of the *Idea of History* have accused Collingwood of attributing too high a degree of rationality and purposiveness to historical actors. Human beings, they claim, are often unreasonable and their actions purposeless. To confine historical enquiry to intentional rational activity is to make it far too intellectualist. *The Principles of History*, however, adds a new dimension. In it Collingwood contends that human beings are only intermittently rational. Unreasonable actions are certainly part of the subject-matter of history. Unreasonable thoughts are just as interesting as reasonable thoughts. Even unreasonable people have reasons, they simply have bad ones. *The Idea of History* was quite rigid in distinguishing between thoughts and feelings. He maintains that emotions are incapable of being re-enacted, whereas thought may be revived time and time again in different contexts. Only thoughts are re-enactable. Emotions and feelings are the context in which thoughts occur. *The Principles of History,* however, severely qualifies this suggestion. In *The Principles of Art*, language as the expression of rational thought does not entirely exclude the emotions. Distinguishing between the essential and the inessential emotions, Collingwood contends, there are necessarily essential emotions implicated in thought and integral to the thoughts of the person performing actions. Hence the rational act of building a fortress may betray the essential emotion of fear, to which the fortification is a response. Collingwood sums up his position by saying that: 'All history is the history of thought. This includes the history of emotions so far as these emotions are essentially related to the thoughts and question; not of any emotions that may happen to accompany them; nor for that matter other thoughts that may accompany them' (Collingwood, 1999: 77).

Conclusion

Since his death Collingwood's reputation has escalated, from a humble revival generated by Alan Donogan and William H. Dray in 1960s to a veritable host of admirers from a wide range of disciplines researching into every aspect of his thought, and finding inspiration for their own work. In 1994 a Charitable Trust was created to promote his life and work, and a Centre established at Swansea University, subsequently translating to Cardiff, to facilitate research into the areas of intellectual activity to which Collingwood contributed. The Centre produces a journal, *Collingwood and British Idealism Studies: incorporating Bradley Studies* (Inglis, 2009: 323)

Bibliography

Ayer, A. J. (1977), *A Part of my Life*. London, Collins.

Ayer, A. J. (1984), *Philosophy in the Twentieth Century*, new edition. London, Routledge.
Boucher, David (1995). 'The Life, Times and Legacy of R. G. Collingwood' in *Philosophy, History and Civilisation*, ed. David Boucher, James Connelly and Tariq Modood. Cardiff: Wales University Press.
Collingwood. J (2012), *A Lakeland Saga: The story of the Collingwood and Altounyan Family in Coniston and Aleppo*. Ammanford, Wales: Sigma Press.
Collingwood, R. G. [1924] (1994). *Outlines of a Philosophy of Art*. Bristol: Thoemmes Press.
Collingwood, R. G. (1932), *Roman Britain*. Oxford: Clarendon Press.
Collingwood, R. G. [1936] (1937), with J. H. L. Myers, *Roman Britain and the English Settlements*, second edition. Oxford: Clarendon Press.
Collingwood, R. G. (1939), *An Autobiography*. Oxford: Clarendon Press.
Collingwood, R. G. [1942] 1992), *The New Leviathan*, revised edition, ed. David Boucher. Oxford: Clarendon Press.
Collingwood, R. G. [1946] (1993), *The Idea of History*, revised edition, ed. W. J. Van der Dussen. Oxford: Clarendon Press.
Collingwood, R. G. (1999), *The Principles of History*, ed. W. H. Dray and W. J. Van der Dussen. Oxford: Clarendon Press.
Collingwood, R and Wright R. 1995 [1965]. *The Roman Inscriptions of Britain*, Vol. 1. Stroud: Alan Sutton.
Collingwood, R. G. (2005) *The Philosophy of Enchantment*, ed. David Boucher, Wendy James and Philip Smallwood. Oxford: Clarendon Press.
Collingwood, W. G. (1893) *The Life & Work of John Ruskin* in 2 volumes. Boston and New York: Houghton Miflin.
Collingwood, W. G. (1907-8), 'A Romano-British settlement at Ewe Close, Crosby Ravensworth', *Transactions, Cumberland and Westmorland Antiquarian and Archaeological Society*, N.S., vols. viii. and ix.
Inglis, Fred (2009), *History Man: The Life of R. G. Collingwood*. Princeton: Princeton University Press.
Toulmin, Stephen (1971), *Human Understanding*, vol. 1. Oxford: Clarendon Press.